Personal Finance for Beginner's - A Comprehensive User Guide

Capiace Wilson

Published by Financierpro Publishing, 2023.

While every precaution has been taken in the preparation of this book, the publisher assumes no responsibility for errors or omissions, or for damages resulting from the use of the information contained herein.

PERSONAL FINANCE FOR BEGINNER'S - A COMPREHENSIVE USER GUIDE

First edition. March 22, 2023.

Copyright © 2023 Capiace Wilson.

ISBN: 979-8215685679

Written by Capiace Wilson.

Financierpro, Publishing

P.O. Box 2266

Antioch, Tn. 37011

enterthecrios@gmail.com

www.financierpro.com

TABLE OF CONTENTS

Introduction

Personal finance is an essential aspect of our lives, and making wise financial decisions can have a significant impact on our financial wellbeing. Unfortunately, many people make foolish assumptions when it comes to personal finance, leading to financial mistakes and missed opportunities. In this chapter, we will explore some of the most common foolish assumptions in personal finance and how to avoid them. One of the most common foolish assumptions in personal finance is that you don't need to budget. Many people assume that they can simply spend money as they see fit and that their finances will work themselves out in the end. However, this is a dangerous assumption, as it can lead to overspending, debt, and financial instability. To avoid this mistake, it's important to create a budget and stick to it. A budget can help you track your spending, identify areas where you can cut back, and ensure that you're saving enough for your future goals. Another foolish assumption in personal finance is that you don't need an emergency fund. Many people assume that they won't experience unexpected expenses or emergencies and that they can simply rely on their credit cards or other forms of borrowing to cover these costs. However, this can lead to high-interest debt and financial stress. To avoid this mistake, it's important to establish an emergency fund. This should be a separate savings account that you contribute to regularly, with the goal of having enough money to cover 3-6 months of expenses. This can help you avoid relying on credit cards or other forms of borrowing in the event of an emergency. Many people assume that they can't invest because they're not wealthy. However, this is a foolish assumption, as anyone can invest regardless of their income or net worth. Investing can be a powerful tool for building wealth over time, and even small amounts of money can grow significantly over the long term. To avoid this mistake, it's important to start investing as early as possible. This can be as simple as investing in a low-cost index fund or using a robo-advisor to manage your investments. By starting early and being consistent with your investing, you can build a substantial nest egg over time. Another foolish assumption in personal finance is that debt is inevitable. Many people assume that they will always have debt and that it's simply a fact of life. However, this is not necessarily true, and carrying high levels of debt can be a major financial burden. To avoid this mistake, it's important to prioritize paying off your debts. This may involve making some sacrifices in the short term, such as cutting back on discretionary spending or taking on extra work. However, by paying off your debts as quickly as possible, you can free up more money to invest in your future goals. Finally, many people make the foolish assumption that their income will always increase over time. While it's certainly possible to increase your income through career advancement or other means, there are no guarantees when it comes to income growth. To avoid this mistake, it's important to focus on building a solid financial foundation. This includes creating a budget, establishing an emergency fund, paying off debts, and investing for your future goals. By focusing on these foundational elements, you can build a strong financial future regardless of how your income may fluctuate over time. Personal finance is a complex and ever-changing field, and there are many foolish assumptions that people make when it comes to managing their money. By avoiding these assumptions and focusing on sound financial principles, you can build a solid financial foundation that will serve you well for years to come. Remember to create a budget, establish an emergency fund, prioritize debt repayment, invest for the future, and focus on building a strong financial foundation that can withstand the ups and downs of life. By doing so, you can avoid costly mistakes, reduce financial stress, and achieve your financial goals over time. It's important to recognize that personal finance is not a one-size-fits-all solution. What works for one person may not work for another, and it's important to tailor your financial approach to your unique circumstances and goals. This may involve seeking the advice of a financial professional, educating yourself on financial principles and strategies, and being open to adjusting your approach as needed. Ultimately, the key to success in personal finance is to stay focused on your goals, remain disciplined and consistent in your approach, and avoid the foolish assumptions that can lead to financial mistakes and missed opportunities. With a clear plan and a commitment to sound financial principles, you can build a solid financial foundation and achieve long-term financial security and success. Personal finance refers to the management of an individual's financial resources, such as income, expenses, savings, and investments. It involves making decisions about how to allocate these resources to meet current and future financial needs and goals. Personal finance is an important aspect of daily life, as it affects many areas of our lives, including our ability to pay for necessities, achieve our long-term goals, and maintain financial stability and security. The basics of personal finance include budgeting, saving, and investing. Budgeting involves tracking and managing your income and expenses and creating a plan to ensure that you're living within your means and saving for your future goals. Saving involves setting aside a portion of your income for emergencies, short-term goals, and long-term goals, such as retirement. Investing involves putting your savings to work to generate returns over time, such as through stocks, bonds, or real estate. Personal finance also involves managing debt, such as credit card debt, student loans, and mortgages. This may involve creating a plan to pay off debts as quickly as possible or refinancing to reduce interest rates and monthly payments. It's important to manage debt carefully, as high levels of debt can have a negative impact on your credit score and overall financial health. Other important aspects of personal finance include insurance, taxes, and estate planning. Insurance helps to protect your finances from unexpected events, such as illness, injury, or property damage. Taxes are an important consideration in personal finance, as they can have a significant impact on your income and overall financial situation. Estate planning involves creating a plan for the distribution of your assets after you die, and may involve creating a will, establishing trusts, and naming beneficiaries for your retirement accounts and other assets. Personal finance is a dynamic field, and it's important to stay informed about changes in laws and regulations, as well as trends in the economy and financial markets. This may involve reading financial news and publications, seeking the advice of a financial professional, or taking courses or workshops to improve your financial knowledge and skills. In addition to the practical aspects of personal finance, there are also emotional and psychological factors to consider. Money is a sensitive topic for many people, and personal finance decisions can be influenced by factors such as fear, anxiety, and social pressure. It's important to be aware of these emotions and to make financial decisions that are grounded in your values and long-term goals, rather than short-term emotions or impulses. Overall, personal finance is an important aspect of our lives, and managing our financial resources effectively can have a significant impact on our overall well-being and quality of life. By staying informed, creating a plan, and making sound financial decisions, we can achieve our financial goals and build a solid financial foundation that will serve us well for years to come. Talking about personal finances with family members at home can be a sensitive and difficult topic. However, it's important to have these conversations to ensure that everyone is on the same page and working towards shared financial goals. When it comes to talking about personal finances with family members, timing is everything. It's important to choose a time and place where everyone is relaxed and not distracted by other activities or responsibilities. Choose a time when everyone is calm and focused and choose a private space where you can talk without interruptions. When it comes to personal finances, honesty is the best policy. Be open and transparent about your financial situation, including your income, expenses, debts, and savings. Encourage other family members to do the same, and work together to identify areas where you can cut back on expenses or increase your income. One of the most important aspects of talking about personal finances with family members is setting shared financial goals. This may involve saving for a family vacation, paying off debt, or investing in a shared asset, such as a home or car. Identify what's important to each family member and work together to create a plan to achieve those goals. Another important aspect of talking about personal finances with family members is discussing financial responsibilities. This may include who will pay for specific expenses, such as rent or groceries, as well as who will be responsible for managing bills and other financial tasks. Be clear about expectations and responsibilities, and work together to ensure that everyone is contributing to the family's financial well-being. If you're having difficulty discussing personal finances with family members, it may be helpful to seek professional help. This may include meeting with a financial planner or advisor, who can provide guidance and support in creating a financial plan that works for your family's unique needs and goals. When talking about personal finances with family members, it's important to be respectful and understanding of each other's perspectives and concerns. Money can be a sensitive topic, and it's important to approach these conversations with empathy and compassion. Avoid blaming or shaming other family members for their financial situation and focus on finding solutions and working together towards shared goals. Finally, it's important to keep communication lines open when it comes to personal finances. Schedule regular check-ins to review your financial situation, discuss progress towards shared goals, and identify any areas where adjustments need to be made. By keeping communication lines open and working together as a team, you can achieve financial stability and security for your family. Talking about personal finances with family members at home can be a challenging but necessary task. By choosing the right time and place, being open and honest, setting shared financial goals, discussing financial responsibilities, seeking professional help if necessary, being respectful and understanding, and keeping communication lines open, you can have productive conversations about personal finances that lead to greater financial stability and security for your family. Financial success is a goal that many of us strive for, but it can be challenging to achieve. There are both real and imaginary hurdles that can stand in the way of our financial success, and overcoming these hurdles requires a combination of knowledge, discipline, and determination. Let's explore some of the most common hurdles to financial success and how to overcome them. One of the biggest real hurdles to financial success is a lack of financial literacy. Many people are not taught the basics of personal finance in school or at home, and as a result, they may struggle to make informed financial decisions. To overcome this hurdle, it's important to educate yourself about personal finance. This may involve reading books or articles, taking courses or workshops, or seeking the advice of a financial professional. Debt is another major hurdle to financial success. High levels of debt can be a significant financial burden, as they can lead to high-interest payments and limit your ability to save and invest. To overcome this hurdle, it's important to prioritize debt repayment. This may involve creating a debt repayment plan, refinancing high-interest debt, or seeking the advice of a financial professional. A limited income can also be a significant hurdle to financial success. It can be challenging to save and invest when you're struggling to make ends meet. To overcome this hurdle, it's important to focus on increasing your income. This may involve seeking a higher-paying job, starting a side hustle, or pursuing additional education or training to increase your earning potential. Unexpected expenses can also be a hurdle to financial success. Emergencies and unexpected costs can throw off your budget and limit your ability to save and invest. To overcome this hurdle, it's important to establish an emergency fund. This should be a separate savings account that you contribute to regularly, with the goal of having enough money to cover 3-6 months of expenses. Fear can be an imaginary hurdle to financial success. Many people are afraid to take risks or make bold financial decisions, such as investing in the stock market or starting a business. To overcome this hurdle, it's important to educate yourself about the risks and rewards of different financial strategies, and to take calculated risks that align with your long-term goals. Self-doubt can also be an imaginary hurdle to financial success. Many people may feel like they don't have the skills or knowledge to achieve financial success. To overcome this hurdle, it's important to believe in yourself and your ability to learn and grow. Remember that financial success is a journey, and it's okay to make mistakes along the way. Procrastination can also be an imaginary hurdle to financial success. Many people may put off important financial tasks, such as budgeting or saving, because they feel overwhelmed or unsure of where to start. To overcome this hurdle, it's important to break tasks down into smaller, manageable steps and to create a plan to achieve your financial goals. Remember that small actions taken consistently over time can lead to significant financial success. Social pressure can also be an imaginary hurdle to financial success. Many people may feel pressure to keep up with their peers or to make financial decisions based on societal expectations rather than their own values and goals. To overcome this hurdle, it's important to stay focused on your own financial goals and to avoid comparing yourself to others. Remember that financial success looks different for everyone, and it's okay to chart your own path. Achieving financial success requires overcoming both real and imaginary hurdles. By educating yourself about personal finance, prioritizing debt repayment, establishing an emergency fund, increasing your income, and taking calculated risks, you can overcome the real hurdles to financial success. To overcome the imaginary hurdles, it's important to believe in yourself, break tasks down into smaller steps, stay focused on your own goals, and avoid comparing yourself to others. Remember that financial success is a journey, and it requires discipline, determination, and a willingness to learn and grow. By taking consistent action towards your financial goals, you can overcome the hurdles that stand in your way and achieve the financial success that you desire. Whether your goal is to save for a down payment on a home, pay off debt, or retire comfortably, with the right mindset and approach, you can make it a reality.

Chapter 1
Avoiding Common Money Mistakes

Managing personal finances can be challenging, especially when there are many financial decisions to make every day. Whether you are new to personal finance or you have been managing your finances for years, it is important to avoid making common mistakes that can lead to financial problems. In this chapter, we will explore some of the most common personal finance mistakes and provide tips on how to avoid them. Overspending is one of the most common personal finance mistakes. Many people spend more than they earn, which can lead to high levels of debt and financial stress. To avoid overspending, it is important to create a budget and stick to it. A budget helps you to track your income and expenses, and it can help you identify areas where you can cut back on spending. Make sure to prioritize your expenses and spend money on necessities first before spending on wants. Another common personal finance mistake is not saving enough. Saving money is crucial for building financial security and achieving long-term goals, such as retirement. To avoid this mistake, make sure to establish an emergency fund to cover unexpected expenses, and prioritize saving for retirement by contributing to a retirement account like a 401(k) or IRA. Aim to save at least 10% to 15% of your income. Debt is a common financial tool that many people use to buy homes, cars, and other big-ticket items. However, taking on too much debt can be a major personal finance mistake. High levels of debt can lead to high-interest payments, which can make it difficult to make ends meet. To avoid this mistake, make sure to only take on debt that you can afford to pay back, and prioritize paying off high-interest debt first. Investing is an important tool for building wealth and achieving long-term financial goals. Many people avoid investing because they are afraid of risk or do not understand how to invest. However, not investing for the future can be a major personal finance mistake. To avoid this mistake, educate yourself about investing and start small. Consider investing in a diversified portfolio of low-cost index funds and aim to hold investments for the long-term.

Retirement is a major financial goal that requires careful planning. Many people make the mistake of not planning for retirement or not starting early enough. To avoid this mistake, start saving for retirement as early as possible, and contribute as much as you can to retirement accounts like a 401(k) or IRA. Consider consulting a financial planner to help you develop a retirement plan that aligns with your goals. Insurance is an important tool for protecting your finances from unexpected events, such as illness, injury, or property damage. Many people make the mistake of ignoring insurance or not having enough coverage. To avoid this mistake, make sure to have adequate insurance coverage for your needs. This may include health insurance, life insurance, disability insurance, and home or renters insurance. Many people make the mistake of not seeking professional help when it comes to managing their personal finances. A financial planner or advisor can provide guidance and support in making important financial decisions and developing a plan for achieving your financial goals. Consider seeking professional help if you feel overwhelmed or unsure about how to manage your finances. Managing personal finances can be challenging, but avoiding common personal finance mistakes can help you achieve financial security and stability. By avoiding overspending, saving enough, managing debt, investing for the future, planning for retirement, prioritizing insurance, and seeking professional help, you can build a solid financial foundation that will serve you well for years to come. Remember that small actions taken consistently over time can lead to significant financial success.

Chapter 2
Understanding Fake Financial Gurus

The rise of the internet and social media has created an environment where anyone can claim to be an expert in any field, including personal finance and investment. As a result, the number of self-proclaimed financial gurus has increased exponentially, making it difficult to differentiate between genuine experts and fake ones. This guide will walk you through the process of recognizing fake financial gurus online, enabling you to make informed decisions and protect yourself from scams. One of the most significant red flags to watch out for when trying to identify fake financial gurus is the presence of unrealistic promises and guarantees. These individuals often claim that they can help you achieve financial success quickly and with little effort. They may promise guaranteed returns on investments or a foolproof way to make money in the stock market. Genuine financial experts understand that there are no guarantees in the world of investing, and making money requires patience, research, and calculated risk-taking. A legitimate financial expert will have the necessary credentials and experience to back up their claims. Look for individuals with certifications such as Chartered Financial Analyst (CFA), Certified Financial Planner (CFP), or Certified Public Accountant (CPA). Additionally, consider their work experience and professional affiliations with well-respected financial institutions or organizations. Fake financial gurus often lack these credentials and may even refuse to disclose their educational background or work experience. Fake financial gurus are known for providing inconsistent or contradictory information. They may frequently change their investment strategies, contradicting previous advice or making claims that are not supported by any evidence. Genuine financial experts maintain a consistent approach to investing and provide well-reasoned advice backed by research and data. Be cautious of those who constantly shift their stance without a justifiable reason. Fake financial gurus often use aggressive sales tactics to push their products or services. They may try to pressure you into making a quick decision by creating a sense of urgency or offering limited-time deals. Legitimate financial experts prioritize your needs and will take the time to understand your financial situation, goals, and risk tolerance before recommending any products or services. They will not pressure you to make hasty decisions. Transparency is a key trait of genuine financial experts. They should be open about their investment strategies, fees, and potential conflicts of interest. Fake financial gurus often lack transparency and may even attempt to hide their true intentions. Be wary of individuals who refuse to disclose their fee structure or provide evasive answers when asked about their investment strategies or potential conflicts of interest. While personal stories can be powerful, legitimate financial experts rely on data, research, and proven methodologies to support their advice. Fake financial gurus often place more emphasis on anecdotal evidence and success stories, rather than providing a solid foundation for their claims. Be cautious of those who rely solely on personal experiences or stories to back up their advice. Fake financial gurus may promote high-risk investments as the key to financial success. While high-risk investments can yield significant returns, they also come with a higher chance of loss. Genuine financial experts understand the importance of a balanced and diversified portfolio, and they will not encourage you to put all your money into high-risk investments without considering your risk tolerance and financial goals. Be cautious of financial gurus who reach out to you unsolicited, especially through email or social media. Legitimate financial experts typically do not use spam or cold calls to generate business. Unsolicited contact may be a sign of a fake financial guru attempting to lure you into a scam or sell you a questionable product or service. Always research the person contacting you and verify their credentials before engaging with them or sharing any personal information. While genuine financial experts may offer their own products and services, they typically maintain a balanced and unbiased approach. Fake financial gurus, on the other hand, may aggressively promote their own products and services while downplaying or dismissing other options. Be cautious of individuals who only advocate for their offerings and do not provide a well-rounded perspective on various financial products and strategies. In today's digital age, a strong online presence is essential for any legitimate financial expert. Research the individual's website, social media profiles, and any available reviews. A poorly designed website, minimal or nonexistent social media presence, and a lack of positive reviews can be warning signs of a fake financial guru. On the other hand, be cautious of overly positive reviews that may have been paid for or falsified. Genuine financial experts will have a mix of positive and negative reviews, as well as a professional online presence. Legitimate financial experts are open to answering questions and addressing concerns. Fake financial gurus may become defensive or evasive when faced with difficult questions or requests for additional information. Be wary of those who avoid answering your questions, provide vague responses, or become defensive when you express doubt or skepticism. Every individual's financial situation and goals are unique, and a legitimate financial expert will recognize this. Fake financial gurus may try to sell a one-size-fits-all approach, claiming that their strategy will work for everyone, regardless of their financial circumstances. Be cautious of individuals who do not take the time to understand your specific needs and tailor their advice accordingly. The internet has made it easier than ever for fake financial gurus to prey on unsuspecting individuals seeking financial advice. By keeping these warning signs in mind, you can protect yourself from falling victim to scams and misinformation. Remember, it is essential to do your research and verify the credentials of any financial expert before trusting their advice or investing your hard-earned money. Always prioritize your financial well-being and seek out reputable, experienced professionals who can provide personalized and well-reasoned guidance.

Chapter 3
Assets, Liabilities, and Net Worth

Understanding the concepts of assets, liabilities, and net worth is essential for anyone looking to take control of their personal finances. These fundamental terms provide the foundation for financial planning, goal setting, and wealth-building. This guide will dive deep into these concepts, helping you understand their importance and how they relate to your overall financial health. An asset is anything you own that has monetary value. Assets can be tangible, like real estate or personal possessions, or intangible, such as investments or cash. There are various types of assets, including: a. Financial Assets - Cash: Money in your checking and savings accounts, or physical cash. Investments: Stocks, bonds, mutual funds, exchange-traded funds (ETFs), and other securities. Retirement Accounts: 401(k)s, IRAs, and other retirement savings vehicles. b. Tangible Assets

Real Estate: The market value of your primary residence, investment properties, or land. Vehicles: Cars, motorcycles, boats, or other modes of transportation.

Personal Property: Jewelry, art, collectibles, and other valuable items. c. Intangible Assets - Intellectual Property: Patents, trademarks, copyrights, and other intangible property rights. Understanding your assets is crucial for financial planning, as they form the basis of your wealth and can generate income or appreciate over time. Increasing your assets is one of the primary ways to grow your net worth.

Liabilities: The Other Side of the Equation - Liabilities represent the debts and financial obligations you have incurred. In personal finance, common liabilities include - a. Short-term Liabilities Credit Card Debt: Balances owed on credit cards. Personal Loans: Unsecured loans borrowed from financial institutions, family, or friends. Medical Debt: Outstanding medical bills. b. Long-term Liabilities Mortgage: The outstanding balance on a home loan. Student Loans: Debts incurred for education purposes. Auto Loans:

Outstanding balances on vehicle financing. Understanding and managing your liabilities is just as important as knowing your assets. Reducing your liabilities can help increase your net worth and improve your overall financial health. Net Worth: The Key Indicator of Financial Health - Net worth is the difference between your total assets and total liabilities. It represents your overall financial position and serves as a snapshot of your wealth at any given moment. Calculating your net worth is relatively simple: Net Worth = Total Assets - Total Liabilities - Understanding your net worth is essential for several reasons: a. Evaluating Financial Health: Your net worth serves as a barometer of your overall financial health, providing a comprehensive view of your assets and liabilities.

b. Setting Financial Goals: By tracking your net worth over time, you can set financial goals and monitor your progress toward achieving them. c. Planning for the Future: A clear understanding of your net worth can help you make informed decisions about retirement planning, debt management, and investing. Increasing Your Net Worth: Strategies for Success - To improve your financial health, it is crucial to focus on increasing your net worth. Here are some strategies to help you achieve this goal: a. Pay Off High-Interest Debt: Prioritize paying off high-interest debts, such as credit card balances or personal loans, to reduce your liabilities and save money on interest payments. b. Save and Invest: Increase your assets by setting aside money in savings accounts, retirement funds, or investment portfolios.

c. Acquire Income-Producing Assets: Consider investing in assets that generate income, such as dividend-paying stocks or rental properties.

d. Limit New Liabilities: Avoid taking on unnecessary debt and practice responsible borrowing habits to prevent your liabilities from growing faster than your assets.

e. Create a Budget: Develop a budget that outlines your income, expenses, and savings goals, helping you to manage your finances more effectively and make informed decisions about your assets and liabilities.

f. Diversify Your Assets: Diversify your investment portfolio by allocating funds across various asset classes, such as stocks, bonds, and real estate. This can help reduce risk and potentially increase your overall net worth over time.

g. Continuously Educate Yourself: Stay informed about personal finance, investing strategies, and market trends to make better decisions about your assets, liabilities, and net worth.

Assessing Your Financial Health: Key Ratios and Metrics

To gain a deeper understanding of your financial health, it is helpful to analyze key financial ratios and metrics. These calculations can provide valuable insights into your current financial situation and help you make better decisions moving forward.

a. Debt-to-Income Ratio: This ratio compares your total monthly debt payments to your monthly gross income. A lower ratio indicates better financial health and a reduced risk of defaulting on your debts.

Debt-to-Income Ratio = Total Monthly Debt Payments / Total Monthly Gross Income

b. Savings Rate: Your savings rate is the percentage of your income that you save or invest. A higher savings rate can contribute to increased net worth over time.

Savings Rate = (Amount Saved or Invested per Month / Total Monthly Gross Income) x 100

c. Asset-to-Liability Ratio: This ratio measures your total assets relative to your total liabilities. A higher ratio indicates a stronger financial position.

Asset-to-Liability Ratio = Total Assets / Total Liabilities

d. Liquid Net Worth: Liquid net worth represents the portion of your net worth that can be quickly converted to cash, providing a clearer picture of your financial stability in the short term. Liquid Net Worth = Total Liquid Assets (Cash, Savings, Investments) - Total Liabilities

Regularly reviewing these financial ratios and metrics can help you assess your financial health, track your progress, and make necessary adjustments to your financial plan. Understanding the concepts of assets, liabilities, and net worth is critical for anyone seeking to improve their financial well-being. By diligently tracking these elements and implementing strategies to increase your net worth, you can work towards achieving your financial goals and creating long-term financial stability. In the journey of personal finance, knowledge is power. Continuously educating yourself and staying informed about market trends, investment strategies, and effective debt management techniques will help you make better decisions and grow your net worth over time. Remember, the key to financial success is a proactive and informed approach to managing your assets, liabilities, and overall financial health.

Chapter 4
Requesting and Fixing Credit Reports in Personal Finance

Credit reports play a crucial role in personal finance, affecting your ability to obtain loans, credit cards, and even employment. Ensuring that your credit report is accurate and up to date is essential for maintaining a healthy credit score and protecting your financial reputation. This guide will provide an in-depth look at the process of requesting and fixing credit reports, empowering you to take control of your credit information and make informed financial decisions. A credit report is a detailed record of your credit history, compiled by credit reporting agencies (CRAs) such as Experian, Equifax, and TransUnion. It contains information about your credit accounts, payment history, outstanding debts, and public records, such as bankruptcies or tax liens. Lenders, creditors, and employers often use credit reports to assess your creditworthiness and financial responsibility. An accurate and positive credit report can help you secure favorable interest rates on loans, qualify for credit cards, and even pass background checks for employment or housing. Under the Fair Credit Reporting Act (FCRA), you are entitled to one free credit report from each of the three major CRAs every 12 months. You can request your credit report through the following channels: a. Online: Visit AnnualCreditReport.com, the only authorized website for free credit reports. Follow the prompts to request your report from one or all three CRAs. b. Phone: Call the Annual Credit Report Request Service at 1-877-322-8228 to request your credit report over the phone. c. Mail: Download and complete the Annual Credit Report Request Form, available on AnnualCreditReport.com. Mail the completed form to:

Annual Credit Report Request Service

P.O. Box 105281

Atlanta, GA 30348-5281

It is a good idea to stagger your requests throughout the year, obtaining one report from each CRA every four months. This strategy allows you to monitor your credit more frequently, ensuring that you are aware of any changes or potential issues. Once you have received your credit report, it is crucial to review it carefully for accuracy. Pay close attention to the following sections: Personal Information: Verify that your name, address, Social Security number, and date of birth are correct. b. Credit Accounts: Ensure that all listed accounts are accurate and up to date. Look for unfamiliar accounts, which could indicate identity theft or fraud. c. Payment History: Confirm that your payment history is accurate, including the status of each account and the dates payments were made. d. Inquiries: Check the list of hard inquiries, which are initiated by lenders when you apply for credit. Ensure that all inquiries are legitimate and that you authorized them. e. Public Records: Review any public records, such as bankruptcies, judgments, or tax liens, to confirm their accuracy. If you discover errors or inaccuracies on your credit report, it is essential to act quickly to dispute them. Errors can negatively impact your credit score and affect your ability to obtain credit or favorable interest rates. Follow these steps to dispute errors on your credit report: Collect any documentation or evidence that supports your claim, such as bank statements, payment records, or correspondence with creditors. Contact the CRA: Write a detailed dispute letter, outlining the specific errors and requesting their removal or correction. Include copies of supporting documentation and your credit report with the errors highlighted. Send the letter via certified mail with a return receipt requested. Contact the Creditor: If the error originates from a creditor or lender, send a similar dispute letter to their address, outlining the specific errors and providing any supporting documentation. Keep a copy of all correspondence for your records. Wait for a Response: Under the FCRA, credit reporting agencies must investigate your dispute within 30 days. They are required to contact the creditor or lender involved and request verification of the information in question. If the information cannot be verified, the CRA must remove or correct the error. Review the Results: After the investigation, the CRA will send you a written response detailing the outcome of your dispute. They may also provide an updated copy of your credit report, reflecting any changes made because of the dispute process. Follow Up: If the error remains on your credit report after the investigation, consider contacting an attorney or filing a complaint with the Consumer Financial Protection Bureau (CFPB). If the error is resolved, continue to monitor your credit report to ensure that it remains accurate and up to date. Taking a proactive approach to managing your credit can help you maintain accurate credit reports and protect your financial reputation. Here are some tips for keeping your credit reports in good shape: Make Timely Payments: Pay your bills on time and in full each month. Late or missed payments can negatively impact your credit score and appear on your credit report. Monitor Your Credit: Regularly request and review your credit reports to ensure their accuracy and identify any potential issues. Maintain Low Credit Utilization: Keep your credit card balances low in relation to your credit limits. High credit utilization can harm your credit score and raise red flags on your credit report. Limit New Credit Inquiries: Avoid applying for multiple credit accounts in a short period, as this can lead to multiple hard inquiries on your credit report and lower your credit score. Protect Your Personal Information: Be vigilant about protecting your personal information to reduce the risk of identity theft, which can result in fraudulent accounts and negative information on your credit report. Requesting and fixing your credit reports are essential aspects of managing your personal finances. By understanding the process and taking a proactive approach to monitoring and maintaining your credit, you can protect your financial reputation and ensure that your credit reports accurately reflect your creditworthiness. Remember, an accurate and positive credit report is key to securing favorable loan terms, qualifying for credit cards, and passing background checks for employment or housing. By staying informed about your credit reports and taking action to correct any errors, you can take control of your financial future and make more informed decisions about your personal finances. Debt is a financial obligation that many people take on to achieve certain goals, such as buying a house, going to college, or starting a business. However, not all debt is created equal. There are two broad categories of debt: bad debt and good debt. What is Bad Debt? Bad debt refers to debt that is incurred to purchase items or services that are not essential and do not have long-term value. Examples of bad debt include credit card debt, car loans, and payday loans. These types of debt tend to have high interest rates and can quickly spiral out of control, leading to financial difficulties. Why is Bad Debt a Problem? Bad debt is a problem because it can lead to financial stress and make it difficult to achieve long-term financial goals. High interest rates and fees associated with bad debt can add up quickly, making it difficult to pay off the debt and causing a cycle of debt that can be difficult to break. Additionally, bad debt does not have long-term value, meaning that the borrower is not investing in something that will appreciate over time. Instead, the borrower is spending money on items or services that will depreciate or provide only short-term benefits. What is Good Debt? Good debt, on the other hand, is debt that is incurred to purchase items or services that have long-term value and can help the borrower achieve their financial goals. Examples of good debt include mortgages, student loans, and business loans. These types of debt tend to have lower interest rates and can provide a significant return on investment over time. Why is Good Debt a Good Investment? Good debt is a good investment because it can help borrowers achieve long-term financial goals. For example, a mortgage can provide a stable and secure place to live, while also appreciating in value over time. Similarly, a student loan can provide the education and training necessary to secure a well-paying job, while also increasing earning potential over time. Business loans can provide the necessary funding to start or expand a business, allowing the borrower to build wealth over time. Good debt is typically associated with investments that appreciate over time, providing a positive return on investment. How to Distinguish Between Bad Debt and Good Debt - Distinguishing between bad debt and good debt can be difficult, as it depends on the individual's financial goals and circumstances. However, there are some general guidelines that can help borrowers distinguish between the two: Consider the interest rate: Bad debt tends to have high interest rates, while good debt tends to have lower interest rates. If the interest rate is high, the debt is more likely to be bad debt. Consider the long-term value: Good debt provides long-term value and can help borrowers achieve their financial goals, while bad debt does not. If the item or service being purchased does not provide long-term value, the debt is more likely to be bad debt. Consider the return on investment: Good debt is typically associated with investments that appreciate over time and provide a positive return on investment. If the investment is not likely to provide a positive return, the debt is more likely to be bad debt. Debt is a financial obligation that many people take on to achieve certain goals. However, not all debt is created equal. Bad debt is debt that is incurred to purchase items or services that are not essential and do not have long-term value, while good debt is debt that is incurred to purchase items or services that have long-term value and can help the borrower achieve their financial goals. By distinguishing between bad debt and good debt, borrowers can make informed financial decisions and work towards achieving their financial goals without becoming trapped in a cycle of debt. While good debt can be a useful tool for achieving long-term financial success, it's important to approach it with caution and only take on debt that is manageable and aligned with your financial goals. Ultimately, by understanding the differences between bad debt and good debt and making informed financial decisions, borrowers can set themselves up for long-term financial success and avoid the pitfalls of excessive debt. Overspending is a common problem that many people face, and it can lead to financial stress and difficulties. However, there are steps that you can take to manage overspending and take control of your finances. The first step in managing overspending is to identify your spending triggers. These are the situations or emotions that cause you to overspend, such as stress, boredom, or social pressure. By understanding your spending triggers, you can develop strategies to avoid or cope with these situations without overspending. Creating a budget is an important step in managing overspending. Start by tracking your income and expenses for a month or two and categorize your expenses into essential and non-essential expenses. Then, set a budget for each category, and be sure to prioritize essential expenses such as rent, utilities, and groceries. Allocate a portion of your income towards non-essential expenses and savings and be sure to stick to your budget. Using cash or a debit card can be a helpful strategy for managing overspending. When you use cash or a debit card, you are limited to spending only what you have, which can help you stay within your budget. Consider leaving your credit cards at home or cutting them up if you find that they are a source of temptation. Setting spending limits can be a helpful strategy for managing overspending. For example, you might set a limit on how much you can spend on dining out or entertainment each month. This can help you stay within your budget and avoid overspending. Impulse purchases can be a major source of overspending. To avoid impulse purchases, consider waiting 24 hours before making a purchase. This can help you determine whether the purchase is truly necessary or if it's just a passing impulse. Shopping with a list can be a helpful strategy for managing overspending. Before you go shopping, make a list of the items you need, and stick to the list. This can help you avoid impulse purchases and stay within your budget. Finding low-cost alternatives can be a helpful strategy for managing overspending. For example, you might consider cooking meals at home instead of dining out, or finding free or low-cost entertainment options instead of spending money on expensive activities. Reviewing your expenses regularly can help you identify areas where you may be overspending. Review your expenses each month and look for areas where you can cut back. Be sure to celebrate your progress along the way and stay motivated to continue managing your overspending. Managing overspending is an important step in achieving financial stability and security. By identifying your spending triggers, creating a budget, using cash or a debit card, setting spending limits, avoiding impulse purchases, shopping with a list, finding low-cost alternatives, and reviewing your expenses regularly, you can take control of your finances and achieve your long-term financial goals. Remember to stay patient and committed and be willing to seek help and guidance when needed. With time and effort, you can manage your overspending and enjoy the benefits of financial freedom and stability.

Chapter 5
Analyzing Your Savings

Analyzing your savings is an important step in managing your finances and achieving your long-term financial goals. By understanding your current savings and identifying areas where you can save more, you can work towards building a solid financial foundation and securing your financial future. In this chapter, we will explore how to analyze your savings and take steps towards improving your financial health. The first step in analyzing your savings is to determine how much you currently have saved. This includes any money you have in savings accounts, investment accounts, retirement accounts, and other financial assets. Make a list of all your savings and investments and calculate the total value. Once you have a clear understanding of your current savings, the next step is to identify your financial goals. This may include short-term goals, such as saving for a vacation or a down payment on a home, as well as long-term goals, such as saving for retirement or paying off debt. Your savings rate is the percentage of your income that you are saving each month. To calculate your savings rate, divide your total monthly savings by your total monthly income. This will give you a percentage that you can use to evaluate your savings habits and identify areas where you can save more. To improve your savings rate, it's important to analyze your expenses and identify areas where you can cut back. Start by tracking your expenses for a month or two and categorize them into essential and non-essential expenses. Look for areas where you can cut back on non-essential expenses, such as eating out, entertainment, or shopping. Creating a budget is an important step in managing your expenses and increasing your savings rate. Start by setting a monthly budget for essential expenses, such as rent, utilities, and groceries. Then, allocate a portion of your income towards non-essential expenses and savings. Be sure to prioritize your savings goals and allocate enough money towards achieving them. Automating your savings is a great way to make sure that you are consistently saving money each month. Set up automatic transfers from your checking account to your savings and investment accounts each month. This will help you stay on track with your savings goals and ensure that you are consistently building your financial foundation. Another important aspect of analyzing your savings is evaluating your investments. Review your investment portfolio and make sure that it is aligned with your financial goals and risk tolerance. Consider diversifying your investments across different asset classes and sectors to reduce risk and increase potential returns. Finally, it's important to re-evaluate your savings plan regularly to ensure that you are on track to achieving your financial goals. Review your savings rate, expenses, and investments regularly, and adjust as needed. Be sure to celebrate your progress along the way and stay motivated to continue building your financial future. Analyzing your savings is an important step in managing your finances and achieving your long-term financial goals. By calculating your current savings, identifying your financial goals, and analyzing your expenses and investments, you can take steps towards building a solid financial foundation and securing your financial future. By creating a budget, automating your savings, and re-evaluating your savings plan regularly, you can stay on track with your financial goals and enjoy the benefits of financial security and stability. Investing can be a powerful way to build wealth and achieve long-term financial goals. However, investing also involves risk, and it's important to have a solid understanding of the market and investing principles before putting your money at stake. Let's explore how to evaluate your investment knowledge and identify areas where you may need to improve your understanding. The first step in evaluating your investment knowledge is to understand basic investment concepts. This includes understanding the difference between stocks, bonds, and mutual funds, as well as understanding the concept of diversification and the role of risk and return in investing. If you are new to investing, start by reading books or online resources on the basics of investing. Another important factor to consider when evaluating your investment knowledge is your risk tolerance. This refers to your willingness to take on risk to achieve higher returns. It's important to understand your risk tolerance and invest accordingly. If you are risk-averse, for example, you may want to focus on more conservative investments, such as bonds or mutual funds, while if you are comfortable with risk, you may be more interested in investing in individual stocks or other high-risk investments. There are many different investment strategies to choose from, each with its own pros and cons. Some common investment strategies include value investing, growth investing, dividend investing, and index investing. It's important to understand the different investment strategies and choose the one that best aligns with your financial goals and risk tolerance. If you already have an investment portfolio, it's important to evaluate it regularly to ensure that it is aligned with your financial goals and risk tolerance. Review your portfolio and make sure that it is diversified across different asset classes and sectors. Consider rebalancing your portfolio if necessary to ensure that it remains aligned with your goals. If you are unsure about your investment knowledge or need help creating a solid investment plan, consider working with a financial advisor. A financial advisor can help you evaluate your investment knowledge, identify areas where you need to improve, and create a customized investment plan that aligns with your financial goals and risk tolerance. Investing is a lifelong learning process, and it's important to continue improving your investment knowledge over time. Read books and articles on investing, attend investment seminars and conferences, and consider taking investment courses or earning professional certifications to improve your skills and knowledge. Finally, it's important to beware of overconfidence when evaluating your investment knowledge. It's easy to become overconfident in your abilities and make risky investment decisions that can lead to significant losses. Stay humble and realistic about your abilities, and always be willing to seek advice and guidance when needed. Evaluating your investment knowledge is an important step in becoming a successful investor. By understanding basic investment concepts, assessing your risk tolerance, understanding investment strategies, evaluating your investment portfolio, considering working with a financial advisor, continuing to learn and improve, and avoiding overconfidence, you can build a solid investment plan that aligns with your financial goals and risk tolerance, and achieve long-term financial success.

Chapter 6
Achieve Financial Goals

Wealth is often defined as the accumulation of assets or financial resources, but this definition is limited and fails to capture the true meaning of wealth. Wealth is a multifaceted concept that encompasses not only financial resources but also personal fulfillment, happiness, and well-being. In this chapter, we will explore how to create your own definition of wealth and achieve true prosperity in your life. The first step in creating your own definition of wealth is to reflect on your values and priorities. What matters most to you in life? What are your long-term goals and aspirations? By understanding your values and priorities, you can create a definition of wealth that is aligned with your personal goals and aspirations. Your life goals are an important factor to consider when creating your definition of wealth. Do you want to travel the world, start a business, or raise a family? Your definition of wealth should be aligned with your life goals and aspirations and should help you achieve the things that matter most to you. Wealth is not just about accumulating financial resources, it's also about personal fulfillment and happiness. Consider what brings you joy and fulfillment in life, and how you can incorporate these things into your definition of wealth. This might include pursuing hobbies or passions, spending time with loved ones, or engaging in meaningful work. Health and well-being are critical components of wealth. Your definition of wealth should prioritize physical and mental health, as well as personal well-being. This might include exercise, meditation, healthy eating habits, or regular self-care routines. Relationships are an important aspect of wealth. Your definition of wealth should prioritize building meaningful relationships with family, friends, and loved ones. Focus on cultivating strong and supportive relationships that bring joy and fulfillment to your life. Giving back to your community is another important aspect of wealth. Consider how you can use your resources and talents to make a positive impact in your community. This might include volunteering, donating to charity, or supporting local businesses. While financial resources are not the only aspect of wealth, they are an important component. Embrace financial freedom by creating a budget, reducing debt, and building a solid financial foundation that supports your goals and aspirations. Finally, cultivating a positive mindset is an important aspect of wealth. Your thoughts and beliefs can have a profound impact on your life, so focus on cultivating a positive and optimistic mindset that supports your goals and aspirations. Practice gratitude, mindfulness, and self-reflection to help you stay focused and motivated. Creating your own definition of wealth is an important step in achieving true prosperity and fulfillment in your life. By reflecting on your values and priorities, considering your life goals, focusing on personal fulfillment, prioritizing health and well-being, building meaningful relationships, giving back to your community, embracing financial freedom, and cultivating a positive mindset, you can create a definition of wealth that aligns with your personal goals and aspirations. Remember to stay committed and focused and be willing to adapt and adjust your definition of wealth as your life circumstances change. With time and effort, you can achieve true wealth and fulfillment in all areas of your life. Building an emergency reserve is an essential step in achieving financial stability and security. An emergency reserve, also known as a rainy-day fund, is a sum of money that you set aside for unexpected expenses or emergencies. The first step in building an emergency reserve is to set a realistic goal. Financial experts recommend having at least three to six months' worth of living expenses saved in your emergency reserve. This includes expenses such as rent or mortgage payments, utilities, food, and other essential living expenses. Calculate your monthly expenses and set a goal for how much you need to save to reach this target. Building an emergency reserve can be daunting, but it's important to start small and be consistent. Begin by setting aside a small amount each month, such as 5% of your income, and gradually increase the amount over time. The key is to make saving a habit and prioritize it as a regular expense in your budget. Automating your savings can be a helpful strategy for building an emergency reserve. Set up a separate savings account and have a portion of your paycheck automatically deposited into this account each month. This can help you save consistently and avoid the temptation to spend the money on non-essential expenses. Windfalls, such as tax refunds or work bonuses, can be a great opportunity to boost your emergency reserve. Consider using a portion of these windfalls to increase your emergency reserve and help you reach your savings goals more quickly. Reducing expenses can be an effective way to increase your savings and build your emergency reserve more quickly. Look for ways to cut back on non-essential expenses, such as dining out or subscription services, and redirect these savings towards your emergency reserve. Your emergency reserve should be a top financial priority, even if it means temporarily delaying other financial goals. Prioritize your emergency reserve and make it a non-negotiable expense in your budget. A high-yield savings account can be a good option for building your emergency reserve. These accounts typically offer higher interest rates than traditional savings accounts, which can help your money grow more quickly over time. Your savings goals may need to be adjusted over time as your financial circumstances change. Revisit your emergency reserve regularly and adjust your savings goals as necessary to ensure that you are on track to achieve your financial goals. Building an emergency reserve is an essential step in achieving financial stability and security. By setting a realistic goal, starting small and being consistent, automating your savings, using windfalls to boost your savings, reducing expenses, prioritizing your emergency reserve, considering a high-yield savings account, and revisiting and adjusting your savings goals, you can build a solid financial foundation that protects you from financial hardship and helps you achieve your long-term financial goals. Remember to stay committed and focused and be willing to adapt and adjust your approach as needed to achieve financial security and stability. Saving money to buy a house or start a business is a major financial goal for many people. It requires discipline, commitment, and a solid financial plan to achieve. The first step in saving money to buy a house is to determine how much you need to save. This will depend on the cost of the house, your down payment, and other expenses such as closing costs and moving expenses. Calculate these costs and set a savings goal that is realistic and achievable. Creating a budget is an important step in saving money for a house. Track your income and expenses for a month or two and categorize your expenses into essential and non-essential expenses. Then, set a budget for each category, and be sure to prioritize essential expenses such as rent, utilities, and groceries. Allocate a portion of your income towards savings and be sure to stick to your budget. Reducing your expenses can be an effective way to increase your savings for a house. Look for ways to cut back on non-essential expenses, such as dining out or subscription services, and redirect these savings towards your house savings fund. Increasing your income can also help you save more money for a house. Consider taking on a side job or freelancing gig to earn extra income, or ask for a raise at your current job. Automating your savings can be a helpful strategy for saving money for a house. Set up a separate savings account and have a portion of your paycheck automatically deposited into this account each month. This can help you save consistently and avoid the temptation to spend the money on non-essential expenses. A high-yield savings account can be a good option for saving money for a house. These accounts typically offer higher interest rates than traditional savings accounts, which can help your money grow more quickly over time. There are a variety of down payment assistance programs available that can help you save money for a house. These programs may provide grants, loans, or other assistance to help you cover your down payment and other expenses. The first step in saving money to start a business is to determine how much you need to save. This will depend on the type of business you want to start, your startup costs, and your ongoing expenses. Calculate these costs and set a savings goal that is realistic and achievable. Creating a business plan is an important step in saving money to start a business. Your business plan should include details such as your business idea, target market, competition, marketing plan, and financial projections. This will help you understand your expenses and create a realistic savings goal. Reducing your expenses can be an effective way to increase your savings for a business. Look for ways to cut back on non-essential expenses, such as dining out or subscription services, and redirect these savings towards your business savings fund. Increasing your income can also help you save more money for a business. Consider taking on a side job or freelancing gig to earn extra income or ask for a raise at your current job. Automating your savings can be a helpful strategy for saving money for a business. Set up a separate savings account and have a portion of your paycheck automatically deposited into this account each month. This can help you save consistently and avoid the temptation to spend the money on non-business expenses. In addition to saving money, you may also consider alternative funding sources such as crowdfunding or small business loans. Crowdfunding platforms like Kickstarter or Indiegogo can help you raise funds from a large group of people, while small business loans from banks or the Small Business Administration can provide capital to help you get started. Business incubators or accelerators can also provide resources and support to help you start your business. These programs typically provide access to mentorship, networking opportunities, and funding resources. Your business savings should be a top financial priority, even if it means temporarily delaying other financial goals. Prioritize your business savings and make it a non-negotiable expense in your budget. Saving money to buy a house or start a business requires discipline, commitment, and a solid financial plan. By determining how much you need to save, creating a budget, reducing your expenses, increasing your income, automating your savings, considering alternative funding sources, prioritizing your savings, and seeking out resources and support, you can achieve your financial goals and build a solid foundation for your future. Remember to stay committed and focused and be willing to adapt and adjust your approach as needed to achieve your financial goals. With time and effort, you can achieve your dreams of owning a home or starting a successful business. Funding a child's education and college is one of the biggest financial commitments that parents can make. It is a long-term investment in their future and requires careful planning and consideration. In this section, we will explore some tips for funding kids' education and college. The earlier you start saving for your child's education, the more time you will have to accumulate savings and take advantage of compound interest. Even if you can only save a small amount each month, starting early can make a big difference in the long run. Determine how much you need to save for your child's education and college expenses, considering tuition, room and board, textbooks, and other expenses. Then, set a savings goal that is realistic and achievable. It's important to keep in mind that college costs may increase over time, so be prepared to adjust your goals accordingly. There are several savings vehicles available for funding kids' education and college, including 529 plans, Coverdell Education Savings Accounts, and custodial accounts. Each option has its own advantages and disadvantages, so it's important to do your research and choose the right option for your family's needs. 529 plans and Coverdell Education Savings Accounts offer tax benefits that can help you save more for your child's education. Contributions to these accounts grow tax-free, and withdrawals for qualified education expenses are also tax-free. Be sure to consult with a financial advisor or tax professional to understand the tax implications of your savings choices. Involving your child in the savings process can help them understand the value of education and motivate them to work towards their own goals. Encourage them to save a portion of their own earnings towards their education and involve them in decisions about which schools to attend and what programs to pursue. Scholarships and grants can help offset the cost of education and reduce the amount of money you need to save. Encourage your child to research scholarship opportunities and consider applying for financial aid through the FAFSA (Free Application for Federal Student Aid). While traditional four-year colleges and universities may be the norm, there are other options to consider, such as community college or vocational schools. These options can be more affordable and offer training for in-demand careers. It's important to be flexible and adapt to changing circumstances when funding your child's education. This may include adjusting your savings goals, exploring alternative education options, or considering part-time work or student loans to cover costs. Funding a child's education and college requires careful planning and consideration. By starting early, setting realistic goals, choosing the right savings vehicle, considering tax benefits, involving your child in the process, looking for scholarships and grants, considering alternative education options, and being flexible, you can create a solid financial plan for your child's future. Remember to consult with a financial advisor and adjust your approach as needed to ensure that you are on track to achieve your goals. With time and effort, you can provide your child with the education and opportunities they need to succeed. Preparing for financial independence and retiring early is a dream for many people. Achieving financial independence means having enough money saved and invested to support your lifestyle without having to work for a living. Retiring early means leaving the workforce before the traditional retirement age of 65. In this section, we will explore some tips for preparing for financial independence and retiring early. The first step in preparing for financial independence and retiring early is to set a realistic goal. Determine how much money you need to support your lifestyle and calculate how much you need to save and invest to achieve that goal. Consider factors such as inflation, taxes, and unexpected expenses. This goal will guide your savings and investment strategies. Creating a budget is an important step in preparing for financial independence and retiring early. Track your income and expenses for a month or two and categorize your expenses into essential and non-essential expenses. Then, set a budget for each category, and be sure to prioritize essential expenses such as housing, food, and healthcare. Allocate a portion of your income towards savings and investments and be sure to stick to your budget. Reducing your expenses can be an effective way to increase your savings and move closer to financial independence. Look for ways to cut back on non-essential expenses, such as dining out or subscription services, and redirect these savings towards your savings and investment goals. Increasing your income can also help you save more money and achieve financial independence. Consider taking on a side job or freelancing gig to earn extra income or ask for a raise at your current job. Investing wisely is a key strategy for achieving financial independence and retiring early. Consider a mix of stocks, bonds, and other assets that match your risk tolerance and investment goals. Be sure to diversify your portfolio to minimize risk. Maximizing your retirement contributions can also help you move closer to financial independence and retiring early. Contribute the maximum amount allowed to your 401(k), IRA, or other retirement accounts, and take advantage of any employer matching contributions. Real estate investments can also be a way to build wealth and achieve financial independence. Consider investing in rental properties or real estate investment trusts (REITs) that generate income and appreciate over time. Creating multiple streams of income can also help you achieve financial independence and retiring early. Consider starting a side business, investing in dividend-paying stocks, or creating passive income streams through rental properties or other investments. Achieving financial independence and retiring early requires discipline and focus. Stay committed to your savings and investment goals and be willing to make sacrifices in the short-term to achieve your long-term goals. Preparing for financial independence and retiring early requires careful planning and consideration. By setting a realistic goal, creating a budget, reducing expenses, increasing income, investing wisely, maximizing retirement contributions, considering real estate investments, creating multiple streams of income, and staying focused and disciplined, you can achieve your financial goals and enjoy a comfortable retirement. Remember to consult with a financial advisor and adjust your approach as needed to ensure that you are on track to achieve your goals. With time and effort, you can achieve financial independence and retire early.

Chapter 7
Dealing With Debt

Using savings to reduce bad debt can be a smart financial strategy for improving your overall financial health. Bad debt is debt that is incurred to purchase items or services that are not essential and do not have long-term value. Examples of bad debt include credit card debt, payday loans, and high-interest personal loans. In this chapter, we will explore some tips for using savings to reduce bad debt. The first step in using savings to reduce bad debt is to evaluate your debt. Determine which debts are considered bad debt and prioritize them based on interest rates and payment terms. High-interest debts, such as credit card debt, should be a top priority. Creating a budget is an important step in using savings to reduce bad debt. Track your income and expenses for a month or two and categorize your expenses into essential and non-essential expenses. Then, set a budget for each category, and be sure to prioritize essential expenses such as housing, food, and healthcare. Allocate a portion of your income towards debt repayment and be sure to stick to your budget. Reducing your expenses can be an effective way to increase your savings and pay down bad debt. Look for ways to cut back on non-essential expenses, such as dining out or subscription services, and redirect these savings towards debt repayment. Increasing your income can also help you save more money and pay down bad debt. Consider taking on a side job or freelancing gig to earn extra income or ask for a raise at your current job. Building an emergency fund is another important step in using savings to reduce bad debt. An emergency fund can help you cover unexpected expenses without resorting to high-interest debt. Aim to save at least three to six months' worth of living expenses in your emergency fund. Once you have evaluated your debt, created a budget, reduced your expenses, and built an emergency fund, it's time to prioritize debt repayment. Make minimum payments on all your debts but put extra money towards high-interest debts first. Consider using the debt avalanche or debt snowball method to accelerate debt repayment. Using savings to pay down debt can be a smart financial strategy, but it's important to use your savings wisely. Avoid depleting your emergency fund or retirement savings to pay down debt. Instead, consider using savings from non-essential expenses or additional income to pay down bad debt. Debt consolidation can also be a helpful strategy for reducing bad debt. This involves taking out a loan with a lower interest rate to pay off high-interest debt. This can simplify your debt repayment and save you money on interest. If you're struggling to manage your debt and savings, consider seeking professional help. A financial advisor or credit counselor can help you create a plan to manage your debt and improve your financial health. Using savings to reduce bad debt can be a smart financial strategy for improving your overall financial health. By evaluating your debt, creating a budget, reducing expenses, increasing income, building an emergency fund, prioritizing debt repayment, using savings wisely, considering debt consolidation, and seeking professional help, you can pay down bad debt and achieve your financial goals. Remember to stay focused and disciplined and be willing to make sacrifices in the short-term to achieve your long-term financial goals. With time and effort, you can reduce bad debt and build a solid financial foundation for the future. Reducing debt when you don't have savings can be a daunting task, but it is possible. It requires a combination of discipline, strategy, and resourcefulness. In this section, we will explore some tips for reducing debt when you don't have savings. The first step in reducing debt when you don't have savings is to prioritize your debts. Determine which debts are considered high-interest debts, such as credit card debt or payday loans. These debts typically have the highest interest rates and should be prioritized for repayment. Creating a budget is an important step in reducing debt when you don't have savings. Track your income and expenses for a month or two and categorize your expenses into essential and non-essential expenses. Then, set a budget for each category, and be sure to prioritize essential expenses such as housing, food, and healthcare. Allocate a portion of your income towards debt repayment and be sure to stick to your budget. Cutting back on expenses can be an effective way to free up money for debt repayment. Look for ways to cut back on non-essential expenses, such as dining out or subscription services, and redirect these savings towards debt repayment. Increasing your income can also help you pay down debt when you don't have savings. Consider taking on a side job or freelancing gig to earn extra income or ask for a raise at your current job. Negotiating with creditors can also be a helpful strategy for reducing debt when you don't have savings. Contact your creditors and explain your situation and ask if they can offer a reduced interest rate or a payment plan that works for your budget. Debt consolidation can also be a helpful strategy for reducing debt when you don't have savings. This involves taking out a loan with a lower interest rate to pay off high-interest debt. This can simplify your debt repayment and save you money on interest. If you're struggling to manage your debt and don't have savings, consider seeking professional help. A financial advisor or credit counselor can help you create a plan to manage your debt and improve your financial health. Even if you don't have savings, there may be opportunities to save money and pay down debt. Consider refinancing your mortgage or car loan to save money on interest or look for ways to save on utilities or insurance. Reducing debt when you don't have savings requires discipline and perseverance. Stay motivated and focused on your debt repayment goals and be willing to make sacrifices in the short-term to achieve your long-term goals. Reducing debt when you don't have savings requires a combination of discipline, strategy, and resourcefulness. By prioritizing your debts, creating a budget, cutting back on expenses, increasing your income, negotiating with creditors, considering debt consolidation, seeking professional help, looking for opportunities to save, and staying motivated and disciplined, you can reduce your debt and improve your financial health. Remember to stay focused on your goals and be willing to make sacrifices in the short-term to achieve your long-term financial goals. With time and effort, you can reduce your debt and build a solid financial foundation for the future. Dealing with credit counselors can be a helpful way to reduce debt and improve financial health. Credit counselors are trained professionals who can provide guidance and support in managing debt and creating a plan for repayment. In this section, we will explore some tips for working with credit counselors and reducing debt. Before working with a credit counselor, it's important to research and compare different credit counseling services. Look for reputable organizations that are accredited by the National Foundation for Credit Counseling or the Financial Counseling Association of America. Check their reviews and reputation with the Better Business Bureau and other consumer advocacy organizations. Credit counseling services may charge fees for their services, so it's important to understand the costs upfront. Look for services that are transparent about their fees and provide a clear breakdown of the costs.

Be wary of services that require payment upfront or make unrealistic promises about debt reduction. Credit counselors will need accurate financial information to provide effective guidance and support. Be prepared to provide information about your income, expenses, debts, and assets. Make sure that all information is accurate and up to date. Creating a budget is an important step in reducing debt and improving financial health. A credit counselor can help you create a budget that prioritizes essential expenses and allocates a portion of your income towards debt repayment. Stick to your budget and avoid unnecessary expenses. Credit counselors can also help you negotiate with creditors to reduce interest rates or develop a payment plan that works for your budget. They may be able to work with creditors to reduce or waive late fees or penalties. Make sure to keep up with the payment plan and communicate with your credit counselor if there are any issues. Debt consolidation can be a helpful strategy for reducing debt and simplifying repayment. This involves taking out a loan with a lower interest rate to pay off high-interest debt. A credit counselor can help you determine if debt consolidation is right for your situation and help you find a reputable lender. Reducing debt requires discipline and commitment to avoid new debt. Avoid using credit cards or taking out new loans unless necessary. Stick to your budget and avoid unnecessary expenses. Reducing debt can be a long and challenging process, but it's important to stay motivated and disciplined. Celebrate small victories along the way, such as paying off a credit card or reducing a high-interest debt. Be willing to make sacrifices in the short-term to achieve your long-term financial goals. Working with a credit counselor can be a helpful way to reduce debt and improve financial health. By researching credit counseling services, understanding the costs, providing accurate financial information, creating a budget, negotiating with creditors, considering debt consolidation, avoiding new debt, and staying motivated and disciplined, you can reduce your debt and build a solid financial foundation for the future. Remember to stay focused on your goals and be willing to make sacrifices in the short-term to achieve your long-term financial goals. With time and effort, you can reduce your debt and achieve financial stability. Filing for bankruptcy is a legal process that can provide relief to individuals and businesses who are struggling with overwhelming debt. However, it is important to understand the pros and cons of filing bankruptcy and the different types of bankruptcy that are available. Discharge of Debt: One of the biggest advantages of filing for bankruptcy is the discharge of debt. This means that some or all your debt will be eliminated, giving you a fresh start. Protection from Creditors: When you file for bankruptcy, an automatic stay is put in place that stops creditors from contacting you or pursuing collection efforts. Repayment Plan: If you file for Chapter 13 bankruptcy, you can create a repayment plan that allows you to repay your debt over time. Improved Credit Score: While bankruptcy can initially hurt your credit score, it can also provide an opportunity for a fresh start and improved credit score over time. Negative Impact on Credit Score: Filing for bankruptcy can have a negative impact on your credit score and can stay on your credit report for up to 10 years. Potential Loss of Assets: Depending on the type of bankruptcy you file; you may be required to sell some of your assets to repay your creditors. Public Record: Bankruptcy is a public record, which means that anyone can access information about your bankruptcy case. Limited Credit Access: After filing for bankruptcy, you may have limited access to credit and may be required to pay higher interest rates. There are several types of bankruptcy that individuals and businesses can file, each with their own requirements and benefits. Chapter 7 Bankruptcy: Chapter 7 bankruptcy, also known as a "liquidation" bankruptcy, is the most common type of bankruptcy filed by individuals. It involves selling non-exempt assets to repay creditors, with any remaining debt being discharged. Chapter 13 Bankruptcy: Chapter 13 bankruptcy involves creating a repayment plan that allows you to repay your debt over a period of three to five years. This type of bankruptcy is often filed by individuals who have a regular income and want to keep their assets. Chapter 11 Bankruptcy: Chapter 11 bankruptcy is typically filed by businesses and involves restructuring debts and assets to repay creditors over time. Chapter 12 Bankruptcy: Chapter 12 bankruptcy is designed for family farmers and fishermen who have regular income but are struggling with debt. Filing for bankruptcy can be a difficult decision, but it can also provide relief to individuals and businesses who are struggling with overwhelming debt. It is important to weigh the pros and cons of filing for bankruptcy and to understand the different types of bankruptcy that are available. By working with an experienced bankruptcy attorney and understanding your options, you can make an informed decision about whether bankruptcy is the right choice for you. Consumer debt can be a challenging and stressful issue to deal with, especially when it comes to stopping the spending cycle that can lead to debt. Many people find themselves caught in a cycle of overspending, accumulating debt, and struggling to make ends meet. The first step in stopping the spending and consumer debt cycle is to identify the problem. This means taking a hard look at your spending habits and understanding why you are overspending. Are you spending to alleviate stress or anxiety? Are you trying to keep up with your peers or portray a certain lifestyle? Are you using shopping as a form of entertainment or distraction? By identifying the root cause of your overspending, you can begin to address the issue. Once you have identified the problem, it is important to create a budget. A budget can help you understand where your money is going and identify areas where you can cut back. Start by tracking your expenses for a month and categorizing them into necessary expenses (such as rent, utilities, and groceries) and discretionary expenses (such as entertainment and dining out). Look for areas where you can cut back, such as reducing your dining out expenses or canceling unnecessary subscription services. Setting financial goals can be a powerful motivator for stopping the spending and consumer debt cycle. Whether your goal is to pay off a certain amount of debt or save for a specific purchase, having a clear goal in mind can help you stay focused and motivated. Set achievable goals and track your progress regularly to stay on track. Avoiding temptation can be a key strategy for stopping the spending and consumer debt cycle. This means avoiding situations that may trigger overspending, such as shopping malls or online shopping websites. If you do need to make a purchase, try to do so with a specific list and avoid browsing or impulse buying. Using cash for purchases can be a powerful tool for stopping the spending and consumer debt cycle. This means using physical cash instead of credit cards or other forms of electronic payment. When you use cash, you are more likely to be mindful of your spending and less likely to overspend. If you are struggling with the spending and consumer debt cycle, it may be helpful to seek help from a financial advisor or credit counselor. These professionals can help you understand your financial situation, create a plan for paying off debt, and develop strategies for managing your finances. Stopping the spending and consumer debt cycle can be a challenging process, but it is an important step towards financial stability and security. By identifying the root causes of overspending, creating a budget, setting goals, avoiding temptation, using cash, and seeking help when needed, you can take control of your finances and break the cycle of debt. With commitment and determination, you can achieve financial freedom and peace of mind.

Chapter 8
Understand Your Taxes

Taxes are a fundamental aspect of modern society and understanding them is important for both individuals and businesses. Taxes provide the government with the revenue necessary to fund public services and infrastructure, and they also play a key role in shaping economic and social policy. In this chapter, we will explore the basics of taxes and how they work. What Are Taxes? Taxes are financial obligations imposed on individuals and businesses by the government. They are used to fund public services and infrastructure, such as schools, roads, and healthcare. Taxes are typically based on income, wealth, consumption, or property. There are several types of taxes that individuals and businesses may be subject to, including: Income Tax: Income tax is a tax on an individual's or business's income. It is typically calculated as a percentage of income earned over a certain period, such as a year. Sales Tax: Sales tax is a tax on goods and services purchased by consumers. It is typically calculated as a percentage of the purchase price and is collected by the seller. Property Tax: Property tax is a tax on the value of real estate and other property. It is typically based on the assessed value of the property and is used to fund local government services. Excise Tax: Excise tax is a tax on specific goods, such as alcohol, tobacco, and gasoline. It is typically included in the price of the product and collected by the seller. Payroll Tax: Payroll tax is a tax on wages and salaries paid to employees. It is typically paid by both the employer and the employee and is used to fund social security and other government programs. How Are Taxes Collected? Taxes are collected by the government through various means, such as: Withholding: Withholding is the process of deducting taxes from an individual's paycheck before it is paid. Employers are typically responsible for withholding taxes from employee paychecks and remitting them to the government. Self-Employment Tax: Self-employed individuals are responsible for paying their own taxes and must file quarterly estimated tax payments. Sales Tax Collection: Businesses that sell goods and services are typically responsible for collecting and remitting sales tax to the government. Property Tax Assessment: Local governments typically assess and collect property taxes on an annual basis. Why Are Taxes Important? Taxes are important for several reasons, including - Funding Public Services: Taxes provide the government with the revenue necessary to fund public services and infrastructure, such as schools, roads, and healthcare. Redistributing Wealth: Taxes can be used to redistribute wealth and promote social and economic equality. Economic Policy: Taxes can be used to shape economic policy, such as incentivizing certain behaviors or discouraging others. Social Policy: Taxes can be used to fund social programs, such as social security and welfare. Taxes are a fundamental aspect of modern society and understanding them is important for both individuals and businesses. By understanding the basics of taxes, including the types of taxes, how they are collected, and why they are important, individuals and businesses can make informed decisions about their finances and contribute to the functioning of society. With ongoing dialogue and collaboration between government and citizens, we can ensure that taxes are fair, effective, and beneficial to all. Employment taxes are a significant expense for both employers and employees. These taxes are used to fund various government programs, such as social security and Medicare. While these taxes are necessary to fund public services and infrastructure, there are ways that employers and employees can reduce their employment tax liability. One strategy for trimming employment taxes is to hire independent contractors instead of employees. Independent contractors are not subject to employment taxes, and employers are not required to withhold taxes or pay employer payroll taxes on their behalf. However, it is important to ensure that the worker is classified correctly as an independent contractor and not an employee to avoid potential legal and tax issues. Employers can also reduce their employment tax liability by offering employee benefits. Certain employee benefits, such as health insurance and retirement plans, are not subject to employment taxes. By offering these benefits, employers can reduce their taxable payroll and save on employment taxes. A Section 125 Plan, also known as a cafeteria plan, allows employees to pay for certain qualified benefits, such as health insurance and dependent care, with pre-tax dollars. By using a Section 125 Plan, both employers and employees can reduce their employment tax liability. Employees can also reduce their employment tax liability by maximizing their retirement contributions. Contributions to qualified retirement plans, such as

401(k) plans, are not subject to employment taxes. By maximizing retirement contributions, employees can reduce their taxable income and save on employment taxes. There are several tax credits available to employers that can help reduce their employment tax liability. For example, the Work Opportunity Tax Credit (WOTC) provides a credit to employers who hire employees from certain targeted groups, such as veterans and ex-offenders. By taking advantage of these tax credits, employers can reduce their tax liability and save on employment taxes. A Professional Employer Organization (PEO) is a third-party provider that handles certain employment functions, such as payroll and benefits administration, on behalf of the employer. By using a PEO, employers can reduce their employment tax liability and administrative burden, as the PEO assumes many of the employer's tax and administrative responsibilities. Trimming employment taxes can be a challenging task, but it is an important step towards reducing costs for both employers and employees. By hiring independent contractors, offering employee benefits, using a Section 125 Plan, maximizing retirement contributions, taking advantage of tax credits, and using a PEO, employers and employees can reduce their employment tax liability and save on taxes. With ongoing dialogue and collaboration between employers, employees, and government, we can ensure that employment taxes are fair, effective, and beneficial to all. Taxes are a necessary part of modern society, but there are ways to reduce the amount of taxes owed. One strategy for reducing taxes is to increase deductions. Deductions are expenses that can be subtracted from taxable income, reducing the amount of income that is subject to taxes. One strategy for increasing deductions is to take advantage of itemized deductions. Itemized deductions include expenses such as charitable contributions, medical expenses, and mortgage interest. By keeping track of these expenses throughout the year, taxpayers can potentially increase their deductions and reduce their tax liability. Contributions to qualified retirement plans, such as 401(k) plans and Individual Retirement Accounts (IRAs), are not subject to taxes until withdrawn. By maximizing retirement contributions, taxpayers can reduce their taxable income and potentially increase their deductions. Business owners and self-employed individuals can potentially increase their deductions by keeping track of their business expenses. Business expenses include expenses such as rent, supplies, and equipment. By keeping accurate records of these expenses, taxpayers can potentially increase their deductions and reduce their tax liability.

Taxpayers can also deduct state and local taxes from their federal income tax. State and local taxes include taxes such as property tax, income tax, and sales tax. By deducting these taxes, taxpayers can potentially increase their deductions and reduce their tax liability. Tax credits are a type of tax incentive that can reduce the amount of taxes owed. Tax credits include credits such as the Child Tax Credit, the Earned Income Tax Credit, and the American Opportunity Tax Credit. By taking advantage of these tax credits, taxpayers can potentially increase their deductions and reduce their tax liability. Charitable contributions are a tax-deductible expense. By donating to charity, taxpayers can potentially increase their deductions and reduce their tax liability. It is important to keep accurate records of charitable contributions, including receipts and documentation of the donation. Increasing deductions on taxes is an effective strategy for reducing the amount of taxes owed. By taking advantage of itemized deductions, maximizing retirement contributions, keeping track of business expenses, deducting state and local taxes, taking advantage of tax credits, and donating to charity, taxpayers can potentially increase their deductions and reduce their tax liability. With ongoing dialogue and collaboration between taxpayers and government, we can ensure that tax policies are fair, effective, and beneficial to all. Investment taxes can significantly reduce the returns on an investment portfolio. It is important to understand the tax implications of various investment strategies and to take steps to reduce investment taxes. One of the most effective ways to reduce investment taxes is to take advantage of tax-advantaged accounts. Examples of tax-advantaged accounts include Individual Retirement Accounts (IRAs), 401(k) plans, and Health Savings Accounts (HSAs). Contributions to these accounts are tax-deductible or made with pre-tax dollars, and the investment earnings are tax-deferred. By contributing to these accounts, investors can reduce their taxable income and potentially reduce their tax liability. Another strategy for reducing investment taxes is to invest in tax-efficient funds. Tax-efficient funds are designed to minimize the tax implications of investing. For example, index funds and exchange-traded funds (ETFs) are often more tax-efficient than actively managed mutual funds because they have lower turnover rates, which reduces capital gains taxes. Tax-loss harvesting is a strategy for offsetting capital gains taxes by selling investments that have decreased in value. By selling these investments, investors can realize capital losses, which can be used to offset capital gains and reduce the tax liability. However, it is important to be aware of the wash sale rule, which prohibits the repurchase of the same or a substantially similar investment within 30 days of the sale. Long-term capital gains are taxed at a lower rate than short-term capital gains. By holding investments for at least one year, investors can potentially reduce their tax liability. This strategy is often used with stock investments, but it can also be applied to other types of investments, such as real estate. Municipal bonds are issued by state and local governments and are often exempt from federal taxes. Some municipal bonds are also exempt from state and local taxes. By investing in municipal bonds, investors can potentially reduce their tax liability. Investors should consult with a tax professional to develop a tax-efficient investment strategy. A tax professional can help investors understand the tax implications of various investments and provide guidance on how to reduce investment taxes. Reducing investment taxes is an important part of developing a successful investment strategy. By taking advantage of tax-advantaged accounts, investing in tax-efficient funds, tax-loss harvesting, holding investments for long-term, considering municipal bonds, and consulting with a tax professional, investors can potentially reduce their tax liability and increase their investment returns. With ongoing dialogue and collaboration between investors and government, we can ensure that tax policies are fair, effective, and beneficial to all. Tax breaks, also known as tax deductions, credits, and exemptions, are provisions in the tax code that allow taxpayers to reduce their tax liability. Tax breaks can be available to both individuals and businesses and are often used to incentivize certain behaviors, such as charitable giving or energy efficiency. The standard deduction is a tax break that is available to all taxpayers, regardless of their income or tax status. The standard deduction allows taxpayers to reduce their taxable income by a set amount, based on their filing status. For example, in 2021, the standard deduction for a single filer is $12,550, while the standard deduction for married filing jointly is $25,100. The standard deduction is a simple and easy way to reduce tax liability for many taxpayers. Charitable contributions are tax-deductible expenses that can be used to reduce taxable income. Taxpayers who donate to qualified charitable organizations, such as non-profits, schools, and religious organizations, can deduct the amount of their donation from their taxable income. Charitable contributions can also provide a sense of satisfaction for individuals who wish to give back to their community. Contributions to qualified retirement accounts, such as 401(k) plans and Individual Retirement Accounts (IRAs), are tax-deductible. These contributions can reduce taxable income and potentially reduce tax liability. Additionally, retirement accounts provide a way for individuals to save for their future and ensure a comfortable retirement. Education expenses, such as tuition and fees, are tax-deductible expenses for both individuals and businesses. Taxpayers who pay for their own education expenses or the education expenses of their dependents can potentially deduct these expenses from their taxable income. Additionally, businesses that provide education benefits to their employees can also receive tax breaks. Taxpayers who make energy-efficient improvements to their home, such as installing solar panels or upgrading insulation, can receive tax credits. These credits can be used to reduce tax liability and encourage the use of sustainable and energy-efficient practices. Businesses can deduct many expenses, such as salaries, rent, and supplies, from their taxable income. By deducting these expenses, businesses can reduce their tax liability and reinvest the savings back into their business. Tax breaks are an important tool for reducing tax liability and incentivizing certain behaviors. The standard deduction, charitable contributions, retirement contributions, education expenses, energy efficiency, and business expenses are just a few examples of tax breaks that are available to individuals and businesses. It is important to understand the tax code and take advantage of the tax breaks that are available. With ongoing dialogue and collaboration between taxpayers and government, we can ensure that tax policies are fair, effective, and beneficial to all.

Chapter 9
Building Wealth Through Investing

Building wealth is a goal for many people. While there are many ways to build wealth, it is important to establish a plan and take deliberate steps to achieve this goal. In this chapter, we will explore some ways to build wealth. One of the most important ways to build wealth is to save and invest consistently. This means setting aside a portion of your income each month and investing it in a diversified portfolio of stocks, bonds, and other assets. By investing consistently over time, you can take advantage of compound interest and potentially grow your wealth over the long term. Debt can be a significant barrier to building wealth. High levels of debt can make it difficult to save and invest and can also increase the risk of financial distress. To build wealth, it is important to minimize debt and pay off any high-interest debt as soon as possible. Increasing your income is another way to build wealth. This can be achieved through a variety of strategies, such as getting a higher-paying job, starting a business, or investing in real estate. By increasing your income, you can have more money to save and invest, which can help you build wealth over time. Many employers offer benefits, such as retirement plans and health insurance, that can help you build wealth. By taking advantage of these benefits, you can save money on taxes and potentially grow your wealth over the long term. A diversified investment portfolio can help you build wealth and manage risk. By investing in a variety of assets, such as stocks, bonds, and real estate, you can spread your risk and potentially earn higher returns over the long term. Building wealth takes time and patience. It is important to focus on long-term goals and avoid making short-term decisions that could harm your financial future. By staying focused on your goals and investing consistently over time, you can potentially build significant wealth over the long term. Building wealth can be complex, and it can be helpful to seek professional advice. Financial advisors and other professionals can provide guidance on investment strategies, tax planning, and other important financial decisions. Building wealth is a journey that requires planning, discipline, and patience. By saving and investing consistently, minimizing debt, increasing your income, taking advantage of employer benefits, building a diversified investment portfolio, focusing on long-term goals, and seeking professional advice, you can potentially build significant wealth over the long term. With ongoing dialogue and collaboration between individuals and professionals, we can ensure that everyone can build wealth and achieve their financial goals. Primary investments are investments made directly into companies or projects, typically in the form of equity or debt. What are Primary Investments? Primary investments are investments made directly into companies or projects, typically during their early stages of development. This type of investment is usually made in the form of equity or debt, and the investor is typically involved in the company's operations and decision-making process. Primary investments can take many forms, including - Venture Capital: Venture capital is a form of primary investment that is typically made into early-stage companies that are looking to grow and scale. Venture capital firms provide funding and other resources to help these companies succeed, and they typically take an ownership stake in the company in exchange for their investment. Private Equity: Private equity is another form of primary investment that is typically made into established companies that are looking to grow or undergo a transformation. Private equity firms provide funding and expertise to help these companies succeed, and they typically take an ownership stake in the company in exchange for their investment. Debt Financing: Debt financing is a form of primary investment that involves providing a loan to a company or project. The investor receives regular interest payments, and the principal amount is repaid at the end of the loan term. How do Primary Investments Work? Primary investments typically involve a high level of due diligence and analysis before an investment is made. Investors will typically perform a thorough analysis of the company or project's financials, management team, market potential, and other key factors before making an investment decision. Once an investment is made, the investor will typically be involved in the company's operations and decision-making process. This involvement can vary depending on the type of investment and the level of ownership stake the investor has in the company. Higher Potential Returns: Primary investments can offer higher potential returns than traditional investments such as stocks and bonds. This is because primary investments are typically made in early-stage companies or projects that have the potential to grow and scale rapidly. Direct Involvement: Primary investments allow investors to be directly involved in the operations and decision-making process of the company or project. This can provide valuable insights and opportunities to influence the direction of the investment. Diversification: Primary investments can provide diversification benefits to an investor's portfolio. By investing in a range of companies or projects, investors can spread their risk and potentially reduce the impact of any individual investment. High Risk: Primary investments are typically higher risk than traditional investments such as stocks and bonds. This is because they are often made into early-stage companies or projects that are not yet established and have a higher risk of failure. Illiquidity: Primary investments can be illiquid, meaning that it may be difficult to sell the investment and receive your capital back in a timely manner. This can make it difficult to manage cash flow and meet other financial obligations. High Capital Requirements: Primary investments typically require a significant amount of capital, making them difficult to access for many investors. Primary investments can offer investors the potential for high returns and direct involvement in the operations and decision-making process of a company or project. However, they also come with higher risks and capital requirements, and may be illiquid. As with any investment, it is important to conduct thorough due diligence and analysis before making a primary investment decision, and to seek professional advice if necessary. Understanding investment returns is an important aspect of investing. Investment returns refer to the gains or losses an investor earns from their investments and can be measured in several ways. There are several types of investment returns, including - Capital Gains: Capital gains are the profits earned from the sale of an asset, such as a stock or real estate. Capital gains are realized when the sale price is higher than the purchase price and are subject to capital gains tax. Dividend Income: Dividend income is the income earned from owning stocks that pay dividends. Dividends are a portion of a company's earnings that are distributed to shareholders and can be reinvested or used for other purposes. Interest Income: Interest income is the income earned from owning bonds or other fixed-income investments. Interest is paid on the principal amount invested and is typically paid at regular intervals. Rental Income: Rental income is the income earned from owning and renting out real estate. Rental income can provide a steady stream of cash flow but is subject to maintenance costs and other expenses. Investment returns can be calculated in several ways, including: Total Return: Total return is the total amount of money earned from an investment over a specified period, including capital gains, dividends, and interest income. Annualized Return: Annualized return is the average rate of return earned on an investment over a specified period, expressed as a percentage. Compound Annual Growth Rate (CAGR): CAGR is a measure of the annual growth rate of an investment over a specified period, considering the effects of compounding. There are several factors that can affect investment returns, including: Investment Strategy: Investment strategy plays a key role in determining investment returns. Different investment strategies, such as value investing or growth investing, may result in different returns depending on market conditions and other factors. Market Conditions: Market conditions can have a significant impact on investment returns. Factors such as interest rates, inflation, and geopolitical events can affect the performance of different asset classes. Diversification: Diversification can help to reduce the risk of investment losses and potentially increase investment returns. By investing in a range of asset classes and sectors, investors can spread their risk and potentially benefit from market growth in different areas. Fees and Expenses: Fees and expenses can reduce investment returns over time. It is important to understand the fees and expenses associated with different investments, and to minimize these costs where possible. Understanding investment returns is an important aspect of investing. Investment returns can be measured in several ways, including total return, annualized return, and compound annual growth rate. Investment returns can be affected by a range of factors, including investment strategy, market conditions, diversification, and fees and expenses. By understanding these factors and taking a long-term approach to investing, investors can potentially achieve their financial goals and build wealth over time.

Chapter 10
Slow and Steady Investments

When it comes to investing, there are many different strategies that investors can use. One popular strategy is the "slow and steady" approach. This approach involves investing in a diversified portfolio of assets over a long period of time. The goal of this strategy is to build wealth over time by taking advantage of the power of compounding. In this chapter, we will explore the concept of slow and steady investments in more detail, discussing the benefits of this approach, the types of assets that are suitable for this strategy, and how to get started with slow and steady investments. Benefits of Slow and Steady Investments - One of the main benefits of the slow and steady approach to investing is that it is a relatively low-risk strategy. By investing in a diversified portfolio of assets over a long period of time, investors can reduce the impact of market volatility on their investments. This is because the performance of different assets tends to be less correlated over longer time periods, meaning that losses in one asset class can be offset by gains in another. Another benefit of the slow and steady approach is that it allows investors to take advantage of the power of compounding. Compounding refers to the process of reinvesting investment gains over time, which can lead to exponential growth in wealth. By investing in a diversified portfolio of assets over a long period of time, investors can benefit from the compounding effect, which can significantly increase their investment returns. Types of Assets Suitable for Slow and Steady Investments: When it comes to slow and steady investments, there are several types of assets that are suitable for this strategy. These include - Stocks: Investing in stocks is a popular way to build wealth over time. Stocks have historically provided higher returns than other asset classes, although they also come with higher risk. To reduce risk, it is important to invest in a diversified portfolio of stocks, such as an index fund or exchange-traded fund (ETF). Bonds: Bonds are a type of fixed-income investment that provides a steady stream of income over time. They are generally less risky than stocks but also provide lower returns. To reduce risk, it is important to invest in a diversified portfolio of bonds, such as a bond index fund or ETF. Real Estate: Real estate is a tangible asset that can provide a steady stream of rental income over time. Real estate investments can include rental properties, real estate investment trusts (REITs), and real estate crowdfunding platforms. Commodities: Commodities are physical assets such as gold, silver, oil, and agricultural products. They can provide diversification benefits to a portfolio and act as a hedge against inflation. How to Get Started with Slow and Steady Investments - Getting started with slow and steady investments is relatively easy. Here are some steps to follow: Set Investment Goals: The first step in any investment strategy is to set investment goals. This includes determining the amount of money you want to invest, the time frame for your investments, and the expected rate of return. Choose Asset Allocation: After setting investment goals, the next step is to determine the appropriate asset allocation for your portfolio. This involves deciding how much of your portfolio should be allocated to each asset class, such as stocks, bonds, and real estate. Diversify Your Portfolio: Diversification is key to reducing risk in your portfolio. By investing in a diversified portfolio of assets, you can reduce the impact of market volatility on your investments. Invest Regularly: One of the keys to the slow and steady approach is to invest regularly over a long period of time. This means making regular contributions to your investment portfolio, whether that be monthly, quarterly, or annually. Rebalance Your Portfolio: Over time, your portfolio may become unbalanced as some assets perform better than others Rebalancing your portfolio is an important step in maintaining a diversified investment strategy. As some assets perform better than others, the overall allocation of your portfolio may become unbalanced, leading to increased risk or missed opportunities. Rebalancing involves selling some of the assets that have performed well and buying more of the assets that have not performed as well, bringing your portfolio back into balance. Here are some tips for rebalancing your portfolio - Set a target allocation: Before rebalancing your portfolio, it is important to determine your target allocation for each asset class. This will help you to determine how much of each asset you should hold in your portfolio. For example, you may decide that you want 60% of your portfolio in stocks, 30% in bonds, and 10% in real estate. Determine your rebalancing frequency: Rebalancing your portfolio too frequently can lead to unnecessary trading costs, while rebalancing too infrequently can lead to an unbalanced portfolio. The frequency of rebalancing will depend on your investment goals and the volatility of the assets in your portfolio. Some investors may choose to rebalance quarterly, while others may rebalance annually. Review your portfolio: Once you have determined your target allocation and rebalancing frequency, you will need to review your portfolio to determine which assets are over or underweight. This can be done by comparing your current allocation to your target allocation for each asset class. Determine which assets to sell: If an asset has performed well and is now overweight, it may be time to sell some of it to bring your portfolio back into balance. On the other hand, if an asset has not performed as well and is now underweight, it may be time to buy more of it to bring your portfolio back into balance. Rebalance your portfolio: Once you have determined which assets to sell and buy, it is time to rebalance your portfolio. This can be done by selling the overweight assets and buying the underweight assets until your portfolio is back in balance. Monitor your portfolio: After rebalancing your portfolio, it is important to continue monitoring it to ensure that it remains in balance. If the performance of your asset's changes, you may need to rebalance your portfolio again to maintain your target allocation. Rebalancing your portfolio is an important step in maintaining a diversified investment strategy. By setting a target allocation, determining your rebalancing frequency, reviewing your portfolio, and rebalancing as needed, you can ensure that your portfolio remains in balance and aligned with your investment goals.

Chapter 11
Mutual Funds and Exchange Traded Funds

Mutual funds and exchange-traded funds (ETFs) are two popular investment options for individuals looking to invest in a diversified portfolio of stocks, bonds, or other securities. Both mutual funds and ETFs offer advantages and disadvantages depending on an investor's goals and risk tolerance. In this chapter, we will discuss the differences between mutual funds and ETFs and the advantages and disadvantages of each. What Are Mutual Funds? Mutual funds are investment vehicles that pool money from multiple investors to purchase a portfolio of stocks, bonds, or other securities. Mutual funds are managed by professional portfolio managers who make investment decisions on behalf of the fund's investors. Mutual funds can be actively managed, meaning the portfolio manager actively buys and sells securities to outperform the market, or passively managed, meaning the fund tracks an index and does not make active investment decisions. Advantages of Mutual Funds - Professional Management: Mutual funds are managed by professional portfolio managers who have the expertise and resources to make investment decisions on behalf of the fund's investors. Diversification: Mutual funds invest in a diversified portfolio of securities, reducing the risk of a single security negatively impacting the fund's performance. Convenience: Mutual funds can be easily bought and sold through a brokerage account or through an investment advisor. Variety: Mutual funds are available in a wide range of investment styles, including growth, value, income, and international, allowing investors to choose a fund that aligns with their investment goals and risk tolerance. Disadvantages of Mutual Funds - Fees: Mutual funds typically charge fees, including management fees, sales charges, and other expenses, which can eat into the fund's returns. Limited Control: Mutual fund investors have limited control over the fund's investment decisions and cannot choose individual securities to invest in. Taxes: Mutual funds may generate taxable capital gains and income distributions, which can increase an investor's tax liability. What Is Exchange-Traded Funds (ETFs)?

Exchange-traded funds (ETFs) are investment vehicles that are like mutual funds but are traded on an exchange like a stock. ETFs are passively managed, meaning they track an index and do not make active investment decisions. ETFs can track a wide range of indices, including broad market indices, sector indices, and international indices. Advantages of ETFs: Diversification: ETFs invest in a diversified portfolio of securities, reducing the risk of a single security negatively impacting the fund's performance. Low Fees: ETFs typically have lower fees than mutual funds, which can lead to higher returns for investors. Flexibility: ETFs can be bought and sold throughout the trading day like a stock, allowing investors to take advantage of short-term trading opportunities. Transparency: ETFs disclose their holdings daily, providing investors with transparency and insight into the fund's investments. Disadvantages of ETFs - Trading Costs: ETFs may incur trading costs, including brokerage fees and bid-ask spreads, which can reduce an investor's returns. Limited Control: ETF investors have limited control over the fund's investment decisions and cannot choose individual securities to invest in. Liquidity: Some ETFs may be illiquid, meaning they may be difficult to buy or sell at a fair price. Mutual funds and exchange-traded funds (ETFs) are two popular investment options for individuals looking to invest in a diversified portfolio of stocks, bonds, or other securities. Both mutual funds and ETFs offer advantages and disadvantages depending on an investor's goals and risk tolerance. Mutual funds are managed by professional portfolio managers and can be actively or passively managed, while ETFs are passively managed and trade like a stock on an exchange. Both mutual funds and ETFs provide diversification, convenience, and variety, but mutual funds may have higher fees and offer limited control, while ETFs may have trading costs and limited liquidity. When deciding between mutual funds and ETFs, investors should consider their investment goals, risk tolerance, and preferences for professional management or control over investment decisions. It is important to research and compare the available options, including fees, performance, and investment strategies, to make an informed decision. Ultimately, the choice between mutual funds and ETFs will depend on the individual investor's needs and preferences. Both options can provide a diversified portfolio of securities and potential returns, but it is important to understand the advantages and disadvantages of each and to choose the option that aligns with your investment goals and risk tolerance.

Chapter 12
Investing in Taxable Accounts

Investing in taxable accounts is a common investment strategy for individuals who want to grow their wealth and earn a return on their investments. A taxable account is any investment account that is subject to taxation on the income or gains generated from the investments held in the account. In this chapter, we will discuss the benefits and drawbacks of investing in taxable accounts and some tips for maximizing your returns while minimizing your tax liability. Benefits of Investing in Taxable Accounts - Liquidity: Taxable accounts are generally more liquid than tax-advantaged accounts such as retirement accounts. This means that you can access your funds more easily if you need to sell your investments or withdraw money. No Contribution Limits: Unlike tax-advantaged accounts such as IRAs and 401(k)s, taxable accounts have no contribution limits. This means that you can invest as much money as you want in a taxable account. Investment Flexibility: Taxable accounts offer more investment flexibility than tax-advantaged accounts. You can invest in a wide range of assets, including individual stocks, bonds, mutual funds, and exchange traded funds (ETFs). Tax Loss Harvesting: Taxable accounts allow you to use tax loss harvesting strategies to offset gains with losses, which can lower your overall tax liability. Drawbacks of Investing in Taxable Accounts: Tax Liability: The biggest drawback of investing in taxable accounts is the tax liability on the income and gains generated from the investments held in the account. You may be subject to capital gains taxes, dividend taxes, and other taxes depending on the investments you hold in the account and your tax bracket. Lack of Tax-Advantaged Growth: Unlike tax-advantaged accounts such as IRAs and 401(k)s, investments in taxable accounts do not grow tax-free. This means that you may pay taxes on the growth of your investments each year, reducing your overall returns. Tips for Maximizing Your Returns in Taxable Accounts: Choose Tax-Efficient Investments: When investing in taxable accounts, it is important to choose tax-efficient investments that generate little to no taxable income or gains. This can include index funds, municipal bonds, and tax-managed funds. Use Tax-Loss Harvesting: Tax-loss harvesting is a strategy that involves selling investments that have lost value to offset gains on other investments in the same account. This can reduce your overall tax liability and increase your returns. Consider Holding Investments for the Long-Term: Holding investments for the long-term can help reduce your tax liability by allowing you to take advantage of lower long-term capital gains tax rates. Keep Good Records: Keeping good records of your investment transactions and tax-related information can help you minimize your tax liability and maximize your returns. Investing in taxable accounts can be a smart investment strategy for individuals who want to grow their wealth and earn a return on their investments. While there are some drawbacks to investing in taxable accounts, such as the tax liability on income and gains, there are also many benefits, including investment flexibility and liquidity. By choosing tax-efficient investments, using tax-loss harvesting strategies, holding investments for the long-term, and keeping good records, you can maximize your returns while minimizing your tax liability in taxable accounts.

Chapter 13
Investing for Educational Expenses

Investing for educational expenses is a smart financial move that can help you save for your or your children's education costs. With the rising cost of education, investing can help you build a college fund and reduce the burden of student loans. In this chapter, we will discuss the different types of investment options available for educational expenses and provide tips for investing effectively. Types of Investment Options: 529 College Savings Plan: A 529 college savings plan is a tax-advantaged investment account designed specifically for education expenses. Contributions to a 529 plan grow tax-free, and withdrawals for qualified educational expenses are also tax-free. Coverdell Education Savings Account (ESA): A Coverdell ESA is a tax-advantaged investment account that allows you to save for qualified education expenses, including K-12 and college expenses. Contributions to a Coverdell ESA grow tax-free, and withdrawals for qualified educational expenses are also tax-free. Custodial Accounts: A custodial account is an investment account in which an adult act as a custodian for a minor. The funds in a custodial account can be used for educational expenses or any other purpose.

Roth IRA: A Roth IRA is a retirement account that allows you to withdraw contributions tax-free at any time. While Roth IRAs are designed for retirement savings, they can also be used for educational expenses without incurring penalties or taxes. Tips for Investing Effectively: Start Early: The earlier you start investing for educational expenses, the more time your investments must grow. By starting early, you can take advantage of compounding interest and potentially save more for educational expenses. Set Realistic Goals: It is important to set realistic goals when investing for educational expenses. Consider the cost of the education you or your children will need and how much you will need to save each year to reach your goal. Diversify Your Investments: Diversifying your investments can help you reduce risk and maximize returns. Consider investing in a mix of stocks, bonds, and mutual funds to spread your risk. Monitor Your Investments: It is important to regularly monitor your investments to ensure they are performing well and to make any necessary adjustments. This can help you maximize your returns and achieve your investment goals. Consider Tax Implications: When investing for educational expenses, it is important to consider the tax implications of your investments. Some investment options, such as 529 plans and Coverdell ESAs, offer tax advantages that can help you save more for educational expenses. Investing for educational expenses is a smart financial move that can help you save for your or your children's education costs. There are several investment options available, including 529 plans, Coverdell ESAs, custodial accounts, and Roth IRAs. By starting early, setting realistic goals, diversifying your investments, monitoring your investments, and considering tax implications, you can maximize your returns and achieve your investment goals. Investing for educational expenses can help reduce the burden of student loans and provide financial security for you or your children's future.

Chapter 14
Investing in Real Estate

Investing in real estate can be a lucrative way to build wealth and generate passive income. Real estate investments offer several benefits, including potential appreciation, steady cash flow, tax advantages, and diversification. In this chapter, we will discuss the different ways to invest in real estate and provide tips for investing effectively. Ways to Invest in Real Estate: Rental Properties: Rental properties are a popular way to invest in real estate. By purchasing a property and renting it out to tenants, you can generate a steady stream of rental income. Rental properties can appreciate over time, providing potential long-term capital gains. Real Estate Investment Trusts (REITs): REITs are investment vehicles that allow investors to invest in real estate without owning physical property. REITs own and manage income-producing properties such as apartment buildings, office buildings, and shopping centers. Investors can earn dividends from the rental income generated by the properties. Real Estate Crowdfunding: Real estate crowdfunding platforms allow investors to pool their money together to invest in real estate projects. This can include investing in individual properties, development projects, or real estate funds. Crowdfunding platforms offer investors access to real estate investments with lower minimum investment requirements. House Flipping: House flipping involves purchasing a property, renovating it, and selling it for a profit. While house flipping can be a high-risk investment strategy, it can also be a lucrative way to generate short-term profits. Tips for Investing Effectively: Research the Market: Before investing in real estate, it is important to research the market to understand trends, demand, and supply. This can help you identify potential investment opportunities and make informed investment decisions. Set Realistic Goals: It is important to set realistic investment goals when investing in real estate. Consider the potential return on investment, the time horizon, and the risk involved in the investment. Build a Strong Network: Building a strong network of professionals, including real estate agents, property managers, and contractors, can help you find and manage investment properties more effectively. Do Your Due Diligence: Before investing in a property, it is important to conduct due diligence to assess the property's condition, rental income potential, and any potential risks. Consider Financing Options: Real estate investments often require significant capital, and financing options can impact your investment returns. Consider different financing options, including traditional mortgages, private loans, or cash purchases, and evaluate the potential impact on your returns. Monitor Your Investments: It is important to regularly monitor your real estate investments to ensure they are performing well and to make any necessary adjustments. This can help you maximize your returns and achieve your investment goals. Investing in real estate can be a lucrative way to build wealth and generate passive income. There are several ways to invest in real estate, including rental properties, REITs, real estate crowdfunding, and house flipping. By researching the market, setting realistic goals, building a strong network, conducting due diligence, considering financing options, and monitoring your investments, you can invest in real estate effectively and achieve your investment goals. Real estate investments offer potential appreciation, steady cash flow, tax advantages, and diversification, making them a valuable addition to any investment portfolio.

Chapter 15
Managing Money and Investments with Technology

Technology has revolutionized the way we manage money, making it easier than ever to keep track of our finances, budget, and invest. There are now a variety of tools and apps available that can help individuals manage their money more effectively, whether it be through budgeting, investing, or tracking expenses. In this chapter, we will discuss the benefits of using technology to manage money and provide some examples of popular apps and tools. Benefits of Using Technology to Manage Money: Convenience: Technology allows individuals to manage their money from anywhere, at any time. With mobile apps and online tools, individuals can monitor their accounts, track expenses, and make investments from the comfort of their own homes. Budgeting: Budgeting apps allow individuals to set financial goals and track expenses to stay on track with their budget. This can help individuals save money and avoid overspending. Investing: Technology has made it easier than ever to invest in the stock market, with apps and online platforms offering low-cost trading and investment options. This has made investing more accessible to individuals who may have been previously intimidated by the stock market. Automation: Technology allows individuals to automate their finances, with features such as automatic bill payment and automatic savings transfers. This can help individuals save time and reduce the risk of missing payments or forgetting to save. Examples of Apps and Tools for Managing Money: Mint: Mint is a budgeting app that allows individuals to track expenses, set financial goals, and receive alerts for overspending. Mint can also be used to monitor credit scores and view investment accounts. Robinhood: Robinhood is a popular investing app that offers commission-free trading for stocks, ETFs, and cryptocurrencies. Robinhood also offers a user-friendly interface and educational resources for beginner investors. Personal Capital: Personal Capital is an investment management platform that offers investment advice and portfolio management services. Personal Capital also offers budgeting tools and a free financial dashboard to track all accounts in one place. Acorns: Acorns is a micro-investing app that automatically invests spare change from transactions into a diversified portfolio. Acorns also offers investment education and retirement savings options. PayPal: PayPal is a digital payment platform that allows individuals to send and receive money electronically. PayPal also offers a variety of financial tools, including budgeting, investing, and credit products. Using technology to manage money can help individuals stay on top of their finances, budget effectively, and invest with confidence. With a variety of apps and tools available, individuals can choose the tools that work best for their needs and financial goals. By taking advantage of the convenience and automation of technology, individuals can save time and money while building a strong financial foundation.

Conclusion

Life changes can have a significant impact on personal finance, whether it be a new job, a marriage, a divorce, or retirement. Each of these life changes can bring unique challenges and opportunities, and it is important to understand how to manage finances effectively during these transitions. In this chapter, we will discuss how different life changes can impact personal finance and provide tips for managing finances effectively. Starting a new job can bring a boost in income, but it can also bring changes in benefits and retirement savings options. Here are some tips for managing finances during a job change: Review Benefits: It is important to review the benefits package offered by the new employer, including health insurance, retirement savings options, and other perks. This can help individuals maximize their benefits and save money on healthcare expenses. Adjust Budget: With a new job and potentially a new income level, it is important to adjust the budget accordingly. This may involve increasing savings, paying off debt, or increasing spending in certain areas. Retirement Savings: If the new employer offers a retirement savings plan, it is important to contribute as much as possible to take advantage of the employer match and save for the future. Marriage can bring changes in income, expenses, and financial goals. Here are some tips for managing finances during marriage: Combine Finances: Couples should discuss whether to combine finances or keep them separate. This can help prevent conflicts over spending and allow for joint financial goals. Create a Joint Budget: Couples should create a joint budget that considers all income and expenses. This can help prevent overspending and allow for savings and debt repayment. Plan: Couples should discuss long-term financial goals, such as saving for a down payment on a house or retirement. This can help ensure that both partners are on the same page and working towards common goals. Divorce can be a challenging time both emotionally and financially. Here are some tips for managing finances during a divorce: Evaluate Assets and Debts: Individuals should evaluate all assets and debts and determine a fair distribution. This may involve working with a financial planner or attorney to ensure that both parties are protected. Budgeting: After a divorce, it is important to create a new budget that considers the new income and expenses. This may involve downsizing, cutting back on expenses, or increasing income through additional work or investment. Retirement Savings: Individuals should review their retirement savings and make any necessary adjustments. This may involve increasing contributions or changing investment strategies. Retirement is a major life change that can bring both excitement and uncertainty. Here are some tips for managing finances during retirement: Review Expenses: It is important to review expenses and adjust the budget accordingly. This may involve downsizing or cutting back on expenses. Retirement Income: Individuals should evaluate all sources of retirement income, including Social Security, pension plans, and retirement savings. This can help ensure that they have enough income to support their retirement lifestyle. Investment Strategy: Individuals should review their investment strategy and make any necessary adjustments to ensure that their investments are aligned with their retirement goals and risk tolerance. Life changes can have a significant impact on personal finance, and it is important to understand how to manage finances effectively during these transitions. By evaluating benefits, creating a budget, and planning, individuals can navigate these changes with confidence and achieve their financial goals. Whether it be a new job, marriage, divorce, or retirement, managing finances effectively is key to a successful financial future. In conclusion, personal finance is an essential aspect of our lives, affecting our financial well-being and overall quality of life. Whether it be budgeting, saving, investing, or managing debt, personal finance requires attention and careful planning. Through effective personal finance practices, individuals can achieve financial stability, build wealth, and achieve their financial goals. Budgeting is a fundamental aspect of personal finance, allowing individuals to track expenses, manage cash flow, and identify areas for savings. By creating a budget and sticking to it, individuals can avoid overspending, reduce debt, and build a strong financial foundation. Saving is another critical aspect of personal finance, providing a cushion for emergencies and helping individuals achieve long-term financial goals such as retirement or buying a home. Through consistent saving practices, individuals can build wealth and achieve financial independence. Investing is an important tool for building wealth and achieving financial goals, whether it be through stocks, bonds, real estate, or other investment vehicles. While investing carries risk, it also provides the potential for long-term returns and can help individuals achieve their financial goals more quickly. Managing debt is also crucial to personal finance, as high levels of debt can impact credit scores and financial stability. By creating a debt repayment plan and managing debt effectively, individuals can reduce debt and improve their financial standing. In addition to these foundational aspects of personal finance, individuals should also consider the impact of life changes on their finances, such as starting a new job, getting married, going through a divorce, or retiring. By understanding how these changes can impact personal finance and taking proactive steps to manage finances effectively, individuals can navigate these transitions with confidence. Overall, effective personal finance practices require discipline, patience, and a willingness to learn and adapt. Through consistent budgeting, saving, investing, and debt management, individuals can build a strong financial foundation, achieve their financial goals, and enjoy a life of financial stability and independence. By taking control of their finances and making informed financial decisions, individuals can create a bright financial future for themselves and their families.